Champions
of Faith

Building Faith Within You

Jimmy R. Stevens

authorHOUSE®

AuthorHouse™
1663 Liberty Drive
Bloomington, IN 47403
www.authorhouse.com
Phone: 1-800-839-8640

Published by AuthorHouse 2/13/2013

ISBN: 978-1-4817-0498-4 (sc)
ISBN: 978-1-4817-0497-7 (e)

Contents

Meet the Writer

Jimmy R. Stevens/Author

- Married to Patricia Stevens and father of Jamie Stevens
- Jimmy Stevens is co-founder with his wife Patricia of Jimmy Stevens Ministries
- He has a B.A. degree in Speech Communications from McNeese State University in Lake Charles, Louisiana
- Post graduate studies at New Orleans Baptist Seminary in New Orleans, Louisiana
- Doctor of Ministry from Lake Charles Bible College
- Gave Pastoral Leadership to the Zion Tabernacle Baptist Church in Lake Charles, Louisiana for nineteen years
- President of Lake Charles Bible College.
- Founding Pastor of the New Covenant Faith Church in Lake Charles, Louisiana
- Author of Books:
  - "Your Riches in Christ"
  - "The Adventure of Faith"
  - "New Beginnings"
  - "Harvest Power"
  - "Strength Like an Eagle"

E-Mail: jrstev22@hotmail.com

Introduction

The 2012 Summer Olympics, XXX Olympiad named the London 2012 were held in London England. There were 204 nations from around the world that participated in this major international colossal and spectator sporting event. Many gold metal champions emerged to name a few, Jamaican sprinter Usain Bolt, swimmer Michael Phelps, gymnast Gabby Douglas, sprinter Allyson Felix, tennis player Serena Williams, and basketball Team USA Coby Bryant and LeBron James. These persons performances were magnificent feats of strength, speed, endurance, agility, skill and inner drive. They are champions in their professional fields of sports. They inspire millions around the world and serve as role models to a younger generation.

Hebrews 11 identifies several biblical champions of the faith who endured great obstacles, barriers, challenges, to defeat and conquer the enemies of their generation. These patriarchs and matriarchs of the faith lives are transitional examples of those who believed in the God of possibilities. As you will study these biblical champions you will be able to build the faith champion that is within you. Through Christ Jesus God has endowed each and every one of us as believers with the extraordinary strength as over comers. May this study build increasing faith within you and ignite you with the audacity to strive to make your God given dreams a reality. Dr. Benjamin Mays said, "Every man and woman is born into the world to do something unique and something distinctive and if he or she does not do it, it will never be done. It must be borne in mind that the tragedy of life does not lie in not reaching your goal. The tragedy of life lies in having no goal to reach. It isn't a calamity to die with dreams unfilled, but it is a calamity not to dream, it is not a disgrace to not reach the stars, but it is a disgrace to have no stars to reach. Not failure, but low aim is sin." Let the words in these pages stir you up to reach the stars in the heavenlies. And may you receive new, fresh insights into God's word and may you never be the same. Look unto Jesus the author and finisher of your faith and then look deep within you and allow the faith champion that you are to emerge. Let Jesus Christ live his life through you working in you both to will and do of his good pleasure.

Background

The Book of Hebrews:

Author Warren W. Wiersbe says, "The Epistle to the Hebrews is a book we need today. It was written at a time when the ages were colliding and when everything in society seemed to be shaking. It was written to Christians who were wondering what was going on and what could they do about it. The stability of the old was passing away, and their faith was wavering.

One of the major messages of Hebrews is-BE CONFIDENT! God is shaking things so that you may learn to live by faith and not by sight. He wants you to build your life on the permanence of the eternal and not the instability of the temporal."

Historical Background:

Authorship: One of the great mysteries surrounding the Book of Hebrews concerns its authorship. The author remains anonymous to us. Suggestions for authors include: Luke, Barnabas, Silas, Apollos and Paul. Most agree that the Apostle Paul is the author.

Circumstances of the Content: The Jewish Christians were experiencing increased persecution. Many of them were growing weary and others of them wanted to go back to their religious traditions of Judaism (animal sacrifices, priest offered sacrifices and lighting of candles, etc.) But the writer wanted these believers to grow in maturity in Jesus.

Personal Applications of the Text: When times get tough for us and when we want to go back to our old ways and comfort zones we have the power of faith. We can be assured that through Jesus he is able to see us through difficult and demanding times as we **"Live by Faith."**

1

The Adventure of Faith
Lesson: Hebrews 11:1-3
Objective: Learning to live by faith

"Without faith it is impossible to please him; for he that cometh to God must believe that he is, and that he is a rewarder of them that diligently seek him." (Hebrews 11:6)

Introduction

Just about every fan of the sport of baseball knows about Cooperstown, New York. This is a little town in New York where the Baseball Hall of Fame is located. There you will find Hank Aaron's uniform, Jackie Robinson's bat and a multitude of other displays. In one section of the building is a collection of plaques honoring all those considered worthy of induction into the Hall.

We see in the word of God that there is a Biblical Hall of Fame of persons that did not center their achievement on human effort but on faith in what God can do! The members of God's Hall of Fame are marked by their confidence in a God that could do the impossible. The bible makes it clear that faith is the essential ingredient of the Christian life. This being the case, it is important that we consider exactly what faith is and began to live by this Spiritual dynamic. This dynamic living will produce an exciting adventure that will propel you from the natural into the life that truly pleases God.

What is Faith?

Hebrews 11:1 is one of the most familiar verses in the New Testament because it gives an answer to the very important question: What is faith? This verse consists of two descriptive phrases, **"Now faith is the substance of things hoped for"** and **"the evidence of things not seen."**

These two phrases are roughly parallel in meaning, but not exactly.

Faith does not float haphazardly in space waiting to be bottled and analyzed. Faith has substance. It bleeds when we cut it. For faith is able to exist only in the shape of a human being. It is a word with a face. Even more, faith is a power with ability to transform human faces. Faith transforms the face of despair into hope, the face of fear into courage, and the face of timidity into boldness. Faith erases the lines of worry and anxiety that wrinkles our lives, and leaves us confident and serene.

It is by faith that our sins are forgiven and we are restored to a right relationship with God. It is by faith that we are delivered from the penalty and power of sin. It is by faith that people whose lives have been shattered by despair, anxiety, and loneliness are reclaimed, repaired, and resurrected through the power of God.

Now Faith Is

Notice that faith is described in the present tense, **"Now."** Faith operates in the present reality even though you may be believing for something that has not even manifested as of yet. Faith takes hold as if it is already in possession. **"Now faith is"** is a right now living reality.

Substance (Confidence)

The word **"substance"** can refer to a strong assurance or confidence in something. Just believing in something is really **"faith in faith"**. But biblical faith is not the assurance or confidence in something "faith in faith" but in someone (our faith is in God). The biblical idea of hope is very different from the world's conception, which is often defined as a desperate, against all odds clinging to the notion that things might turn out all right. But the believer's hope is built on the promises of God and His redeeming purpose.

We have hope because we are certain that God is trustworthy and good. This **"hope"** that we have can be defined as **"expectation"**. So faith is the expectation (hope) that what you are believing will come to pass. This **"hope"** gives birth to a strong assurance or confidence. This confidence is what the word calls **"substance"**. Faith puts confidence in the Almighty God (The Promiser) who is able to perform what ever He promises.

Romans 4:21, "And being fully persuaded that, what he (God) had promised, he was able also to perform."

Romans 4:21, "Fully satisfied and assured that God was able and mighty to keep His word and to do what He had promised.

Evidence (Inner Conviction)

Like **"substance"** or confidence, the word "evidence" can refer to proof or to the strong conviction (inner conviction) that arise in the presence of such proof. In a court of law the judge wants "evidence" or proof on the case. You can't go by hear-say or a thought-so, but by the evidence or proof. So a person of faith believes in unseen realities as much as if they were visible to his physical eyes. These unseen realities are things that are of eternal value. Therefore biblical faith means that we live in the confidence of the promises of God through His word. The word of God gives us both the **"assurance"** (confidence) and **"evidence"** (inner conviction) that God will do what He says that He will do.

Numbers 23:19, "God is not a man, that he should lie; neither the son of man, that he should repent: hath he said, and shall he not do it? Or hath he spoken, and shall he not make it good?"

There are three components that relate to three aspects of our humanness-intellect, emotion, and will. Faith speaks to what we believe, how we feel, and what we do. The Bible affirms that all three components-how we believe, feel, and act-are vital to a complete understanding of faith.

Faith as Belief

The first aspect of faith is intellectual. Faith involves the intellect. The Bible calls this belief. We believe that those things in the Bible are true. For the Christian, faith as belief means to be convinced intellectually that those historical events and spiritual concepts declared in the Bible are true. Faith is not a blind leap in the dark, but is rather based on solid evidence, the evidence for us is the word of God.

Faith as Feeling

Faith also involves our emotions. Since God has created us as emotional beings it is right for our feelings to be responsive to Him. Faith develops within an inner confidence or inner conviction that whatever we are standing on will be manifested. Because we respond to God faith is manifested as trust.

Faith as Action

The third thing that distinguishes saving faith from "useless" faith (James 2:20) is the action of faith. Saving faith involves our will to commit to doing God's will. Hebrews 11 illustrates what it means to have faith, in example after example of people who acted on what they believed and then obeyed the God they trusted.

- "By faith Abel offered to God a better sacrifice than Cain, through which he obtained the testimony that he was righteous" (v.4).
- "By faith Noah, being warned by God about things not yet seen, in reverence prepared an ark for the salvation of his household, by which he condemned the world, and became an heir of the righteousness which Is according to faith" (v.7)
- "By faith Abraham , when he called, obeyed by going out to a place which he was to receive for an inheritance; and he went out, not knowing where he was going" (v.8).
- "By faith Abraham, when he was tested, offered up Isaac" (v.17).
- "It was faith that made Moses, when he had grown up, refuse to be called the son of the king's daughter. He preferred to suffer with God's people rather than to enjoy sin."

We see real faith in action. Abel's faith led him to make an offering. Noah's faith motivated him to spend 120 years building an enormous boat in the middle of a desert. Abraham's faith caused him to pack up all of his belongings, leave the town where he grew up, and head for a place he knew nothing about. By faith Moses, turned his back on the good life in the palaces of Egypt and chose instead to identify in suffering with the oppressed people of Israel. Faith that saves is faith that has action.

Elders Obtained a Good Report

The author points out that faith was what God was looking for throughout Old Testament history. The text says in Hebrews 11:2, **"For by it (faith) that the elders obtained a good report." Elders** here refer here to the Old Testament ancestors (People like Abel, Enoch, Noah, Abraham, Sarah and others). Faith was the means by which these ancestors **"obtained a good report"** or were declared to be righteous in the sight of God. It was by faith that these ancestors received God's approval. God was looking for a people who would believe that He existed and take Him at His word. Today God is looking for those who would by faith believe in Jesus Christ and receive God's acceptance and approval. It is through Jesus that we are declared righteous.

II Corinthians 5:21, "For he hath made him to be sin for us, who knew no sin; that we might be made the righteousness of God in him."

Ephesians 1:3, "Blessed be the God and Father of our Lord Jesus Christ, who hath blessed us with all spiritual blessings in heavenly places in Christ."

Faith Framed the Worlds

The word says in, "Hebrews 11:3, "Through faith we understand that the worlds were framed by the word of God, so that things which are seen were not made of things which do appear." The world and the vast universe in which we live were created by our God. All the planets, stars, the sun and moon, the oceans, lakes and mountains were all created by him.

Psalm 8:3, "When I consider thy heavens, the work of thy fingers, the moon and the stars, which thou hast ordained."

Psalm 19:1, "The heavens declare the glory of God; and the firmament sheweth his handywork."

Genesis 1:1, "In the beginning God created the heavens and the earth.

It is through faith that we believe and understand that this universe was created by God. We cannot explain it all and we cannot even explain the existence of God. But we do believe it by faith. Remember that our "substance" or confidence is because of the "evidence" or proof. We trust in the word of God. His word "framed" the worlds the things that we see and enjoy were made of things invisible. What an incredible God that we worship and serve.

Questions & Answers

1) What is faith to you?

_____

_____

_____

_____

2) What does the word substance mean?

_____

_____

_____

_____

3) What are you presently hoping for?

_____

_____

_____

_____

4) What does evidence mean?

_____

_____

_____

_____

5) Have you received the inner evidence?

_____

_____

_____

_____

2

A Faith that Worships With Excellence

Lesson: Hebrews 11:4
Objective: Learning to worship God with excellence

"By faith Abel offered unto God a more excellent sacrifice than Cain, by which he obtained witness that he was righteous, God testifying of his gifts: and by it he being dead yet speaketh." (Hebrews 11:4)

Introduction

In the Biblical Hall of Faith our first hero that is chronicled is Abel. Abel was a worshipper. As a worshipper he only wanted to worship God with the sacrifices of excellence. He unselfishly offered himself and the very best that he had. His worship was pleasing to God and it became a sweet aroma in the nostrils of the Almighty God. Have you come to the place where you are the kind of worshipper that is committed to excellence? God seeks true worshippers who will worship Him in spirit and in truth.

Profile of Abel

Strengthens and Accomplishments:

- First member of the Hall of Faith in Hebrews 11
- First Shepherd

- First Martyr for Truth
- Lived just outside of Eden
- Relatives: Parents:

Lessons from his life

- God hears those who come to Him in faith
- Relatives: *Parents*: Adam and Eve, *Brother*: Cain

Key Verses

- Abel's story is told in Genesis 4:1-8; He is mentioned in Matthew 23:35; Luke 11:51; Hebrews 11:4 and 12:24

In the life of Abel we learn how faith connects us to God in worship. You and I have been created to worship. Abel was a worshipper who received the approval of God because by using his faith he offered sacrifices of excellence. We can take Abel's example at heart and daily connect with the Living God whose name is, "Excellent".

A Faith that Produces Excellence
Hebrews 11:4, "By faith Abel offered unto God
a more excellent sacrifice than Cain."

In Genesis 4:1-10, we have the account of Adam and Eve's two sons, Cain and Abel. The central truth of these verses is that God is to be worshipped, that He is to be worshipped by means of a sacrifice, and that He is to be worshipped by means of a sacrifice which is appropriated by faith. Abel was a shepherd and Cain was a farmer. There came a time in which both Abel and Cain brought unto God an offering as an expression of worship. Worship is our response to God by honoring, blessing and giving unto Him.

"And in the process of time it came to pass, that Cain brought
of the fruit of the ground an offering unto the Lord. And
Abel, he also brought of the firstlings of the flock and of the
fat thereof. And the Lord had respect unto Abel and to his

offering. But unto Cain and to his offering he had not respect.
And Cain was very wroth, and his countenance fell."
(Genesis 4:3-5)

Both Abel and Cain brought an offering to God. Abel being a shepherd brought the firstlings of his sheep unto the Lord and Cain being a farmer brought of the fruit of the ground (fruit and vegetables) as an offering unto the Lord in worship. But the word of God says that the Lord accepted Abel and his offering but God rejected Cain and his offering! Did Cain bring to God leftovers? Was there a difference in Cain's personality? Was there any character defect in Cain? What made the difference between Cain and Abel was in their worship. Our text says, **Hebrews 11:4, "By faith Abel offered unto God…"**

It was the faith factor! Abel's faith expressed itself in the way he offered his sacrifice unto the Lord. Abel offered his gifts unto the Lord with excellence. He gave a more excellent sacrifice than his brother Cain. It was by faith that Abel offered unto God his worship. He offered unto God first himself. First of all, we must offer ourselves as living sacrifices.

Romans 12:1, "I beseech you therefore, brethren by the mercies of God, that ye present your bodies a living sacrifice, holy, acceptable unto God, which is your reasonable service." (KJV)

Romans 12:1, "Therefore, I urge you, brothers, in view of God's mercy, to offer your bodies as living sacrifices, holy and pleasing to God – this is your spiritual act of worship. (NIV)

II Corinthians 8:5, "And this they did, not as we hoped, but first gave their own selves to the Lord."

Abel offered unto the Lord a more excellent sacrifice than Cain. The sacrifice that Abel offered unto the Lord was marked as being "more excellent" than Cain's sacrifice. This word excellence is defined as the state of excelling or being superior. Abel's offering was superior or it was a better sacrifice than Cain. There are at least four reasons that Abel's offering was superior to Cain's offering.

1) **Because it was an act of faith:**
   Hebrews 11:4, "By faith Abel offered unto God…"

2) **Because it was an act of obedience:**
   Hebrews 11:4, "By faith Abel obeyed God and brought an offering that pleased God more than Cain's offering did."(Living Translation)
   No doubt God gave specific instructions in how He wanted the sacrifice to be made unto Him. God gives instructions and set standards according to His word.

3) **Because Abel brought the firstlings of his flock:**
   Genesis 4:4, "And Abel, he also brought of the firstlings of his flock…"

4) **Because Abel's offering was a blood sacrifice:**
   Genesis 4:4, "And Abel, he also brought of the firstlings and of the fat thereof."
   Hebrews 9:22, "….and without shedding of blood there is no remission (forgiveness)"

A Faith that Gets the Approval of God
Hebrews 11:4, "By faith Abel offered unto God a more excellent sacrifice than Cain, by which he obtained witness that he was righteous, God testifying of his gifts…."

Abel offered unto God by faith and obedience the firstlings of his flock. The firstlings of his flock were all the firstborn. But he also offered the fat thereof also, Abel pleased God and won God's approval. One of the great struggles in the life of the believer is our striving to win the approval of others. We should always strive to seek the approval of God. The scripture says that Abel, "obtained witness that he was righteous." God declared Abel to be a righteous man because Abel's sacrifice pleased God. And because God declared Abel to be righteous God was testifying that Abel's gifts and worship unto Him pleased Him.

When Cain realized that Abel's offering was accepted and his offering was rejected, he became very angry. Cain had worked hard and labored as a farmer. The gifts that he brought was from the ground that he had toiled but still perhaps Cain's attitude was improper or his offering was not up to the God's standards. God evaluates both our motives and quality of what we offer Him. But the Lord approached Cain gave him a second chance to right his wrong and try again to offer a worship that would be pleasing to Him. But Cain's anger gave way to jealousy for his brother Abel.

But unto Cain and to his offering he had not respect. And Cain was very wroth, and his countenance fell. And the Lord said unto Cain, Why art thou wroth? And why is thy countenance fallen? If thou doest well, shalt thou not be accepted? And if thou doest not well, sin lieth at the door. And unto thee shall be his desire, and thou shalt rule over him. (Genesis 4:5-7)

But on Cain and his offering he did not look with favor. So Cain was very angry, and his face was downcast. Then the Lord said to Cain, "Why are you angry? Why is your face downcast? If you do what is right, will you not be accepted? But if you do not do what is right, sin is crouching at your door, it desires to have you, but you must master it." (Genesis 4:5-7, NIV)

God identified for Cain the raging emotion of anger at the door of his heart. God used the word "crouching" to let Cain know that his anger was like a wild animal ready to pounce on him. God also encouraged Cain that he could master his anger by simply doing what was right. If Cain would do what was right then he and his offering would be accepted.

A Faith that Impacts for Eternity
Hebrews 11:4, "By faith Abel offered unto God a more
excellent sacrifice than Cain, by which he obtained
witness that he was righteous, God testifying of his
gifts: and by it he being dead yet speaketh."

Rather than Cain deal with what was wrong in the way he worshipped God and offered sacrifices, he allowed the anger in his heart to master him. His anger gave way to jealousy and Cain murdered his brother Abel. But even though Abel's innocent blood was shed in that field. His blood from the ground cried out to God. Although Cain tried to silence Abel, he continued to speak. His life had made an impact for generations to come. Because Abel had used his faith in an excellent way he still is impacting people right now today.

God desires that your life as a believer will impact others for eternity. When we witness and lead others to Christ we have just impacted a soul for eternity. Can you imagine that one day we will all stand before the Lamb that was slain for us and praise His wonderful name. By faith Abel's life still speaks to us today. He speaks to all believers that it is by our faith that we truly worship and please God. When we worship and minister to others we should offer excellence. Excellence in our living and giving. Excellence is the only way to get the job done!

Questions & Answers

1) Can you honestly characterize your worship as being with excellence?

_____

_____

_____

_____

2) Are you being obedient in your giving unto God?

_____

_____

_____

_____

3) Are you dealing with any anger and unforgiveness with any person?

_____

_____

_____

_____

4) Are you willing to be more sacrificial in your worship?

_____

_____

_____

_____

3

A Faith that Pleases God
Lesson: Hebrews 11:5-6
Objective: Learning how to please God

By faith Enoch was translated that he should not see death; and was not found, because God had translated him: for before his translation he had this testimony, that he pleased God. But without faith it is impossible to please him: for he that cometh to God must first believe that he is, and that he is a rewarder of them that diligently seek him. (Hebrews 11:5-6)

Introduction

We live in a time in the Christian community where there are so many mixed signals concerning the teaching on the subject of faith. As Christians in large we are being made to believe that faith is only designed to get us bigger cars, larger houses and more material stuff. Very seldom do we hear that our faith is designed to please God. In our lesson today we will learn from a man who walked with God and had a testimony that he pleased God. I believe that this should be our chief goal and objective as believers in Jesus Christ

Profile of Enoch

Strengthens and Accomplishments
- Lived before the flood
- The father of Methuselah

- A witness for God in a corrupt society
- Prophesied concerning the second coming of Jesus
- Genealogy: Seventh from Adam
- Lived 365 years
- Never died but was translated into heaven

Lessons from his life

- We can have close fellowship with God
- We can truly please God by the life we live

Key Verses

- Enoch's story is told in Genesis 5:21-24; He is mentioned in Hebrews 11:5 and Jude 14, 15.

The Faith Revelation and Consecration
Hebrews 11:5, "By faith Enoch…"

In Genesis chapter 5: 21-24, we have the account of a man named Enoch. At the age of sixty-five years old his son was born. Enoch received a divine revelation because the name of his son, Methuselah means, "when he is dead it shall be sent." It appears that God was going to preserve the world from judgment (the flood) as long as Methuselah would live. It also appears that Enoch received this divine revelation from God by faith and that this was the means of leading him into a close fellowship with God.

Genesis 5:22, "And Enoch walked with God after he begat Methuselah three hundred years…"

Enoch is one of but two men of whom it is said in scripture that he "walked with God." The days in which Enoch lived on the earth were wicked. It seems that Enoch stood alone in his fearless denunciation of the ungodly. His name means "consecrated." To be consecrated means to be set-apart for a divine purpose or use. It was Enoch's faith in God and what God had revealed to him that consecrated him and truly pleased God.

Jude 1:14-15, "Enoch, the seventh from Adam, prophesied about these men: "See, the Lord is coming with thousands upon thousands of his holy ones to judge everyone, and to convict all the ungodly of all the ungodly acts they have done in the ungodly way, and of all the harsh words ungodly sinners have spoken against him."

From the book of Jude we can see that Enoch was a preacher who saw the ungodly of his day do and say things that was contradictory of God's word. The actions of his generation displeased God. He also saw the impending judgment of God coming unto God's people. Whether he received the revelation of a world-wide flood we do not know. But what we do know about Enoch was that he consecrated himself unto the Lord so that his life would be pleasing unto God.

II Timothy 2:20-21, "But in a great house there are not only vessels of gold and silver, but also of wood and of the earth; and some to honor, and some to dishonor. If any man therefore purge himself from these, he shall be a vessel unto honor, sanctified, and meet for the master's use, and prepared unto every good work."

Through Enoch's faith he set himself apart to be used by God unto his generation. You and I should make a commitment afresh to consecrate ourselves unto the Lord. With this new commitment you will be able to do the great work of God effectively.

The Faith Walk
Hebrews 11:5, "By faith Enoch"
Genesis 5:2, "And Enoch walked with God..."

For three hundred years, Enoch grew into close communion and fellowship with God. The scriptures call it, "walking with God." Fellowship is an interesting word in the Greek language. It comes from the word "koinonia" which means intimate relationship. Each day Enoch learned to speak to and hear from God. Today we speak to God by prayer. Prayer is communication with God. God desires that prayer be not only a monologue but a dialogue with Him.

Each day God eagerly awaits for you to come before Him, praise Him and receive your daily provisions from Him. Also God desires that you open up his word so that He can speak to you. And that you respond in faith and obedience concerning His will for your life. This is what is called, **"having fellowship with God."**

As we began to have growth in the knowledge of God we began to know Him. It is quite a difference in knowing about Him and knowing Him on a personal level. I believe that the reason the scripture notes that Enoch walked with God for three hundred years is because God wants us to be aware that this Christian life is progressive (we grow each day). Our walk with God can produce a lifestyle that will be pleasing to God.

Faith's Testimony
Hebrews 11:5, "By faith Enoch...had this
testimony, that he pleased God."

At the end of Enoch's three hundred years of his spiritual journey with God, he had the testimony that he pleased God. One of the great struggles is when we live just to please others and especially to please our selves. Many therapists tell us today that many people suffer from what they label as "Pleasers." Pleasers are people who suffer emotional pain, and deep bondage from living their lives only from the perspective of others and self. This inner pain comes from the root cause of not feeling "acceptance" and "love". Compounded by a poor self image and feelings of inferiority a pleaser lives in an emotional prison. But God desires that we live balanced lives and that we break free today and live to please Him.

Galatians 1:10, "For do I now persuade men, or God? Or do I seek

to please men? For if I yet pleased men, I should not be the servant of Christ."

To become a balanced Christian is to began to know who you are in Christ through his word (Ephesians chapter 1 is a great text on our identity in Christ). A Christ-centered identity begins when you know that you are accepted because of Jesus Christ. Enoch lived truly to please God in whatever he did. You and I can do that also!

Faith's Reward
Hebrews 11:5, "By faith Enoch was translated that he should not see death; and was not found, because God had translated him:"

After Enoch lived on earth for three hundred and sixty-five years, God took him to Himself, as if to show that he was an example of a human being who had fulfilled his destiny. The scripture says that, "God translated him." Because he walked with God when other men were walking away from Him, he daily came nearer to him into the very presence of God with whom he had always walked.

Enoch walked with God, and how can two walk together accept they agree. We can conclude that Enoch walked in complete obedience to God to the revealed will of God. What joy he must have brought to the heart of God. He lived so close to God that suddenly God translated him from this life. One moment he was here, and the next moment he was gone! He avoided the experience of physical death. Also Enoch's translation is a type of every believer's "rapture" from the earth when Jesus comes back again. This is called the rapture of the church. The Lord Jesus will descend from Heaven into the air to catch up to Himself His blood bought children.

I Corinthians 15:51-52, "Behold I show you a mystery; we shall not all sleep, but we shall all be changed. In a moment, in a twinkling of an eye...

I Thessalonians 4:17, "Then we which are alive and remain shall be

caught up together with them in the clouds, to meet the Lord in the air: and so shall we ever be with the Lord."

Just as Enoch was translated to heaven without seeing death, so also will those of the Lord's people who remain on earth will be snatched up alive to be with the Lord. Because of Enoch's faith, he brought pleasure to the heart of God and it pleased God. Just like Enoch, it is our faith in Jesus that pleases God. Without faith it is impossible to please God. And so as we come to God we must first believe that He is (He exists). We must believe that He is everything that we need. When we believe that God is all sufficient then we will find out that He will reward us, if we diligently seek Him.

Become a **"God Pleaser"** today. Seek to know and experience God in exciting ways. Consecrate yourself to Him, walk in His word and receive His great rewards of your faith.

Hebrews 11:6, "But without faith it is impossible to please Him: for he that cometh to God must believe that He is (That he exists), and that he is a rewarder of them that diligently seek him."

Questions & Answers

1) Do you wrestle with trying to please other people in your life?

_____

_____

_____

_____

2) What experience in your life where you were let down in trying to please?

_____

_____

_____

_____

3) Describe your walk with God in the area of prayer.

_____

_____

_____

_____

4) Share your testimony in your last spiritual victory!

_____

_____

_____

_____

4

A Faith That Obeys God
Lesson: Hebrews 11:7
Objective: Learning to be obedient and to persevere with God-size assignments

By faith Noah, being warned of God of things not seen as yet, moved with fear, prepared an ark to the saving of his house; by the which he condemned the world, and became heir of the righteousness which is by faith. (Hebrews 11:7)

Introduction

We are called to impact the world around us. Many times we ask the question, "Can one person really make a difference?" In today's lesson we will study about a man who made a difference in his generation. He was a man who in the midst of a decaying society around him was able to model obedience to God. The Almighty God gave to him a long term project that lasted 120 years. He was a man of steel-like conviction, courage and faith. Through his steadfast and unwavering commitment he built the first ship that survived the world-wide flood. His only human passengers on board was his own family (eight in all) but through his family God repopulated the world. This giant of a man will forever be remembered as, "The Model of Consistent Obedience"!

Profile of Noah

Strengthens and Accomplishments

- Great grandson of Enoch
- Grandson of Methuselah
- Only follower of God in his generation
- First major shipbuilder
- Man of patience, consistency, and obedience

Weakness and Mistake

- Got drunk and embarrasses himself in front of his sons

Lessons from his life

- God is faithful to those who obey him
- God does not always protect us from trouble, but cares for us in spite of the trouble
- Obedience is a long-term commitment

Vital Statistics:

- Occupation: Farmer, shipbuilder and preacher

Key Verses:

- Noah's story is told in Genesis 5:29-10:32; He is mentioned in I Chronicles 1:4; Isaiah 54:9; Ezekiel 14:14, 20; Matthew 24:37, 38; Luke 3:36; 17:26, 27; Hebrews 11:7; I Peter 3:20; 2 Peter 2:5

An Uncontaminated Faith in a Contaminated World
Hebrews 11: 7, "By faith Noah…"

In Genesis chapter 6:1-13, we have the description of a society that had become contaminated with evil. The word tells us that there was a population explosion on the face of the earth and that, "The sons of God had married the daughters of men." These "sons of God" and the "daughters of men" were mixed marriages between the godly line of Seth and the ungodly line of Cain. These marriages produced offspring or children that were not brought up in the acknowledgement, fear and reverence of the Almighty God. These children grew to become adults that became men of might and renown but men who governed their society without the restraints of the commandments of God. They were giants in human intellect but they were moral midgets in spirituality. They did not retain God in their knowledge.

Genesis 6: 4-5; 11-12, "There were giants in the earth in those days; and also after that, when the sons of God came in unto the daughters of men, and they bare children to them, the same became mighty men which were of old, men of renown. And God saw the wickedness of man was great in the earth, and that every imagination of the thoughts of his heart was only evil continually the earth also was corrupt before God, and the earth was filled with violence. And God looked upon the earth, and behold, it was corrupt: for all flesh had corrupted his way upon the earth.

The society is described as wicked, evil, corrupt and filled with violence. This sounds like some of the cities in our nation today. Carnal and unspiritual parents had produced carnal and unspiritual children that had given rise to a world that had become morally contaminated. Satan today has contaminated our world with immoral sexual behavior, pornography, drugs, injustice, hatred, terrorism, murder, rape, child abuse and many other demonic devices. We learn that a society like this does not bring neither pleasure nor glory to God is in a spiritual crisis and at the brink of the judgment of God. Matter of fact, the evil of this generation brought pain to the heart of God. Have you ever thought of God being pained by your actions? The word described God as being "grieved" even to the point that He repented that He had made man. What a reality of pain in the Lord's heart!

Genesis 6: 6, "And it repented the Lord that he had made man on the earth, and it grieved him at his heart."

God decided that the only way to rid the earth from this moral contamination was that He had to destroy the world and began anew. But God would call out a remnant for Himself and so as God looked down upon the earth there was only one man who had not been contaminated by the evil of his day. This man was named Noah. There are three important characteristics about Noah's character that caused Noah to find grace in the eyes of the Lord.

Genesis 6: 9, "Noah was a just man and perfect (blameless) in his generations, and Noah walked with God."

A Faith that Takes God at His Word
Hebrews 11:7, "By faith Noah being warned of God...

The Almighty God chose to speak and reveal to Noah His plan to save the world. The entire world both man, fowl, fish and animal would be judged by God. He always chooses to speak to us through His word. God revealed to Noah that He wanted him to build an ark, a ship in the middle of the desert because it would rain. It had never rained before on the earth before and no one had ever built a ship. These instructions were strange indeed but Noah received this word as a "warning" from God and stepped out with faith and reverence for his assignment. He took God at His word. God calls you and I to obey His word regardless of the consequences because His word is true.

Hebrews 11:7, "(Prompted) by faith Noah, being for-warned of God concerning events of which as yet there was no visible sign, took heed..."(Amplified)

Hebrews 11:7, "By faith Noah, when warned about things not yet seen, in holy fear..."

Genesis 6: 13, "And God said unto Noah, The end of all flesh is come before me; for the earth is filled with violence through them; and, behold I will destroy them from the earth."

Noah was warned by God of things not yet seen! Remember that Noah had not yet seen rain, nor yet seen a flood and nor yet seen at ship. But by faith he took God at His word.

A Faith that Moves into Action
Hebrews 11:7, "By faith Noah, being warned of God
of things not seen as yet, moved with fear..."

Faith is an action word. Faith motivates us to do something. Faith releases us to move out of our comfort zone into adventurous action. When Noah heard the word of God He moved with fear. He was awed by God's direction and he stepped out to accomplish the task before him. I'm sure that this task was awesome to him but he decided to obey God's will for his life. God instructed Noah to build an ark. The ark was not Noah's idea but it was all God's directives! God carefully detailed to Noah all the specifications needed to build the ark from the building materials, to sizes of the door and window. Through God's word He as given to us all of the specifications to building victorious Christian lives. The word gives us instructions how to build a marriage, financial success and godly living. Are you being obedient to Him? If not, it's time to move into action.

Genesis 6: 14-16, "So make yourself an ark of cypress wood; make rooms in it and coat it with pitch inside and out. This is how you are to build it: The ark is to be 450 feet long, 75 feet wide and 45 feet high. Make a roof for it and finish the ark to within 18 inches of the top. Put a door in the side of the ark and make lower, middle and upper desks." (Living Word)

The ark project would not be a short-term commitment. This ark would have to be prepared. Sometimes we believe that because we are walking in faith that we don't need to plan. But the old adage says, "When you fail to plan you plan to fail." Noah prepared this ark by the plans that God gave to him. From every yard of the ark to every inch was carefully designed by God. We need to be always people of preparation. He prepared the ark even to the saving of his house. Everyone else on the entire earth was destroyed but Noah and his entire family was saved. If no one else receives salvation in your circle of influence, you should make every effort for the saving of your house.

2 Peter 2:5, "And spared not the old world, but saved Noah the eighth person…"

The ark is a type of Jesus. The ark represents the safety and security that is found in the salvation that Jesus provides on the cross. Noah had a faith that moved in action. He was building a godly family as he was building the ark.

A Faith that Testifies to the World
Hebrews 7: By faith Noah, warned of God of things not seen as yet, moved with fear, prepared an ark to the saving of his house; by which he condemned the world.

Noah's faith in building the ark testified of his obedience to God to an unbelieving world. Can you imagine that Noah began to build the ark in the desert. He was miles from any river or ocean but yet he continued to build on the instructions that God gave to him. As he build this strange looking ship; the people mocked, laughed and scorned him, especially when he preached about the judgment of God to come by the way of the flood. Noah preached the word of righteousness. But Noah remained faithful to this project! Noah built on the ark for one-hundred and twenty years. This was a long time commitment. For these one-hundred and twenty years God was also patient in extending His invitation of repentance.

1 Peter 3:20, "Which sometime were disobedient, when once the longsuffering of God waited in the days of Noah, while the ark was a preparing, wherein few, that is, eight souls were saved by water."

2 Peter 2:5, "And spared not the old world, but saved Noah the eighth person, a preacher of righteousness, bringing in the flood upon the world of the godly.

Noah remained dedicated to his assignment. He never wavered and he never doubted that the ship that he was building was the provision for the unsaved world. Finally when it began to rain, the rain was a testimony that Noah had heard from God. Let your life and let your commitment to your assignment to a witness to the world that you are indeed a child of the living God.

A Faith that Receives the Righteousness of God
Hebrews 11: 7, "By faith Noah, warned of God of things
not seen as yet, moved with fear, prepared an ark to the
saving of his house; by the which he condemned the world,
and became heir of the righteous which is by faith.

It was because of Noah's faith that he became an heir of the righteousness of God. An heir is one who is a beneficiary of the possession of another. The most prized possession of God is his righteousness. Because of our faith in Jesus Christ the Lord imputes his righteousness to us. The word "impute" is a banking term that means to put to one's account. We through faith have had the righteousness of God imputed to us. And because of God's righteousness we become the heirs of God's spiritual riches. Noah and his family rode through the greatest storm in the history of mankind but God preserved them. And when it was over, Noah and his family stepped out to a new beginning and continued on the journey of faith. It is through our obedience that we also step out to our new beginning.

Questions & Answers

1) What assignment do you think that God has given to you?

_____

_____

_____

_____

2) What resources do you need to carry out your assignment?

_____

_____

_____

_____

3) What kinds of opposition that you are coming against?

_____

_____

_____

_____

4) How are you going to use your faith in completing your assignment?

_____

_____

_____

_____

5

A Faith that is An Adventure
Lesson Hebrews 11: 8-11
Objective: Learning that faith can
be an exciting adventure

By faith Abraham, when he was called to go out into a place which he should after receive for an inheritance, obeyed: and he went out, not knowing whither he went. (Hebrews 11:8)

Introduction

When I was a teenager there was an exciting television show called "Star Trek" which starred Captain Kurk, his first commander named Mr. Spark and the space crew. They traveled in the space ship "Enterprise" which speed through the star lighted galaxy making all types of discovery on different planets. Although this show was a fiction, it was very exciting for me to tune in each week and watch Captain Kurk and his crews' space exploration. They brought about the discovery and learning of new adventures. As Christians our faith walk with God can be an exciting adventure. The faith of Abraham was so powerful that he is called, "The father of all who believe."

Profile of Abraham

Strengths and Accomplishments

- Became the founder of the Jewish nation
- His faith pleased God

- Was respected by others and courageous in defending his family
- Was a successful and wealthy rancher

Weakness and Mistakes:

- Under direct pressure, he distorted the truth

Lesson from his life:

- God desires dependence, trust, and faith in him-not faith in our ability to please him

Vital Statistics:

- Born in the Ur of the Chaldeans; spend much of his life in the land of Canaan

Key Verse

"And be believed the Lord, and the Lord reckoned it to him as righteousness". His story is told in Genesis 11-25.

A Faith that is Ready for Adventure
Hebrews 11:8, "By faith Abraham, when he was called to go..."

The call of Abram came to him when he was seventy-five years in his country. His father, Terah was an idol god maker and worshipper. But God had something on His mind! He was going to build a nation of people, a special people who would be His very own. And so He calls out Abram to be His vessel.

Genesis 12:1, "Now the Lord had said unto Abram, get thee out of thy country, and from thy kindred, and from thy father's house, unto a land that I will shew thee."

God summons to Abram meant that he had to leave home and family and business; yet he went. He had to go into the unknown, but yet he went. He had to go without a map, but yet he went. By faith Abram took God at His word! Sometimes we wonder what would happen to us if we took God at His word and act on His promises. Can you imagine the faith it took for Abram and his wife Sarah to step out on the promises of God.

If faith can be seen every step of the way, it is not faith. It is necessary for us to take the way to which the Voice of God is calling us. It is always easier for us when we have to walk in familiar territory. But sometimes God calls us out of our comfort zone to the adventure of trusting him to lead us day by day. To Abram, this call was not something that he dreaded. But by faith, he excitedly decided to move with God. Are you ready for the adventure of moving with God? Just as God called Abram away from his family, friends and comfortable surroundings, He is doing the same right now. Yes it is sometimes scary but as long as we know that it is God that is leading us, we are confident that everything will be alright.

Hebrews 11:8, "By faith, Abraham, when he was called to go out into a place which he should after receive for an inheritance, obeyed; and he went out, not knowing where he was going."

The thing that pleased God was that Abraham obeyed him. Although he took his father Terah and his nephew, Lot with Him, he obeyed God by moving out. He took the Lord at His word and walked out, even though he didn't know all the details. Knowing all the details makes some journeys seem to be **easier**, but Abram didn't have all the details. Abram had God's promise. Let this journey be an exciting adventure for you!

The Faith that is Patient
Hebrews 11:9, "By faith he sojourned in the land of promise..."

When Abram did reach the land of promise, he was never allowed to possess it. He had to wander in it, a stranger and a tent-dweller. Yet he never abandoned his faith. God promised Abraham a son and he had to wait for twenty-five years. By faith he was patient, even though he acted in the flesh when he took Hagar, his maid as his wife. But yet God knew that Abraham was going to believe even though physically his body was dead.

Abram sojourned in the land of promise because he never allowed himself to be permanently attached to one place. One of our problems is that we are always in a hurry. To wait is even harder than to adventure. The hardest time is always the time in between. This is the time that the enemy attacks us with his darts of doubt and fear. The person of faith will continue to believe because God settles that person upon the rock of endurance.

I Peter 5: 10, "But the God of all grace, who hath called us unto his eternal glory by Christ Jesus, after that ye have suffered a while, make you perfect, establish, strengthen and settle you."

Faith has a way of completing, establishing, strengthening and settling you. Faith has a way of taking away the anxiety, restlessness and worry. Abraham became established in the conviction that God would do what He had promised to do. You need to stop all your worrying because God will perform His promises.

Romans 4: 20, "He (Abraham) staggered not at the Promise of God through unbelief; but was strong in faith, giving glory to God."

His patience gave way to a strong faith!

Romans 4:21, "And being fully persuaded that, what He (God) had promised, he was able to perform."

A Faith Which Looks Beyond This World
Hebrews 11: 10, "For he looked for a city which hath foundations, whose builder and maker is God."

Any person who has ever did anything great has always had a vision which enabled him to face the difficulties and discouragements of the way. God gave to Abraham a burning vision of a city. He could see this city where God Himself was the architect, builder and maker. It was this heavenly vision that motivated and inspired Abraham. Abraham knew that this world was not his home, so he was at ease to live in tents and to dwell in a strange country. For right now we are like Abraham. We are dwelling in this temporary place. But we are encouraged because we know that better is coming to us; not only in this life but in the life to come. So our faith must look beyond our present circumstances to the glorious rewards that await us. Use your faith to look beyond today because by faith we know that tomorrow it will be brighter. Abraham took joy in knowing that his journey was an adventure of faith.

A Faith that Believes in the Impossible
Hebrews 11:11, "Through faith Sarah herself received strength to conceive seed, and was delivered of a child when she was past age, because she judged him faithful who had promised."

When Sarah first heard that she would get pregnant, she laughed because a ninety year old woman would have a baby. Sometimes in hearing the promises of God, the human reaction is often that this is too good to be true. For Abraham and Sarah having a baby was humanly impossible. But by the grace and power of God, the impossible can become possible. Men spend the greater part of their lives putting limitations on the power of God. Our text tells us that it was through faith that Sarah received the strength to conceive seed. And she delivered a child when she was past age. Nothing is past age with God. Sarah received this strength because she judged God to be faithful. We may be unfaithful but God is faithful to do what He has promised. He promised it and He delivered it in His own time and in His own way. God challenges you and me to have the "God-Kind of Faith" to believe the impossible.

"All things are possible, if we only believe"

Questions & Answers

1) Is your faith journey presently exciting to you?

_____

_____

_____

_____

2) Are you excited about finding out truths in the word?

_____

_____

_____

_____

3) What fears are you willing to confront in the future?

_____

_____

_____

_____

4) What areas do you need patience as you are believing God?

_____

_____

_____

_____

6

A Faith that Focuses on the Future
Hebrews 11:13-19
Objective: Learning how to move on
to the future and seeing that there
are better things awaiting you

And truly, if they had been mindful of that country from whence they came out, they might have had opportunity to have returned. But now they desire a better country, that is, a heavenly: wherefore God is not ashamed to be called their God: for he hath prepared for them a city. (Hebrews 11:15-16)

Introduction

It is interesting how little eaglets learn how to fly. The Mother Eagle lovingly and carefully builds a nest with sticks, twigs and soft grass. The nest becomes a home both for her and her little eaglets. The little eaglet lives in the comfortable nest paddled with soft and warm grass. The eaglet grows very comfortable in its new environment. It is said that when the time comes for the little eaglet to fly, that the Mother Eagle begins to remove the soft grass out of the nest, only leaving the sticky branches and twigs. This strategy is very significant because it is designed for the little eaglet to become uncomfortable.

This uncomfortable reality of the branches and sharp sticks pricks the little eaglet to the point that the little eaglet jumps out of the nest. But what the little eaglet doesn't realize is that the Mother Eagle is watching all the time. As the little eaglet falls through the air trying to fly the Mother eagle comes and scoops up the little eaglet, until the eaglet flies on its own.

There are times in our lives that the Lord stirs up our nests so that He might move us out of our comfort zones. Our move out of the nest is not designed by the Sovereign God for us to fall helplessly to the earth and crash but that we may learn as the little eaglet to mount up on our consecrated faith wings and that we may be able to soar above our difficulties and challenges. God does that so that He can bring us into our true destiny. Sometimes He even allows painful experiences to transpire in our lives so that He can move us out of our comfortable nests. But in all, He is moving us into His great promises. Today we will continue with the story of Abraham who teaches how to not to be trapped by our past but move forward into the bright future by faith.

A Faith that Takes Hold of the Promises of God
Hebrews 11:13, "These all died in faith, not having received the promises, but having seen them afar off, and were persuaded of them, and embraced them, and confessed that they were strangers and pilgrims on the earth."

The old patriarchs are recorded as not having received the promises in their lifetime but they saw the promises and lived in hope of the promises. They were fully persuaded, they embraced them in faith and they lived detached from the things on this earth that binds us to a life of mediocrity. They even considered themselves as strangers and pilgrims passing through this earth. This mindset allowed them to perform tremendous miracles and even to die for what they believed.

Today we have the complete revelation of Gods' word through the Holy Bible, we have the power of the Holy Spirit within us and we have the High Priestly ministry of Jesus Christ in Heaven. But we are often times limited by how we think. We have never been completely transformed with the "God-Kind" of thoughts that takes the limitations off of an Infinite and Almighty God. We seem to be tied down by the restrictions of this carnal humanist society.

Romans 12:2, "Don't become so well-adjusted to your culture that you fit into it without even thinking. Instead fix your attention on God. You'll be changed from the inside out. Readily recognize what he wants from you and quickly respond to it. Unlike the culture around you always dragging you down to its level of immaturity, God brings the best out of you, developing well-formed maturity in you." (Message Translation)

Romans 12:2, "Do not be conformed to this world-This age, fashioned after and adapted to its external, superficial customs. But be transformed (changed) by the (entire) renewal of your mind-by its new ideals and its new attitude..." (Amplified)

But we are challenged to live by the word of God (the promises). We are to be fully persuaded, we are to fully embrace the word and even daily verbally confess the word of God.

Matthew 4:4, "But He replied, It has been written, Man shall not live and be upheld and sustained by bread alone, but by every word that comes forth from the mouth of God." (Amplified)

A Faith that is Determined to Go Forward
Hebrews 11:14-16, "For they that say such things declare
plainly that they seek a country. And truly, if they had
been mindful of that country from whence they came out,
they might have had opportunity to have returned. But
now they desire a better country, that is heavenly:"

Abraham lived in the Ur of the Chaldeans. This city was situated on the Euphrates River, halfway between the head of the Persian Gulf and Baghdad, in present day Iraq. At this time the City of Ur was at the height of its splendor. The city was a prosperous center of religion and industry. It was a tremendous advanced cultured place. Abraham father, Terah owned a successful business of manufacturing and selling of idol god statures which produced for this family material wealth.

When Abraham received the call from God to leave his country, leave his family and friends; he was perhaps giving up a comfortable lifestyle of the rich and famous to travel across the country to find another land. He was a city person adapting to live in the country dwelling in tents and moving from place to place. Now this was a great adjustment in his life. He had lived in one of the most cultured and advanced cities of his day. He had lived there all of us life. But now God calls him to uproot and began a walk of faith.

There will be times in our lives that God will call us to leave a familiar environment (our family, relatives and friends) and move out with Him into an unfamiliar place. Now how do you deal with moving forward? First of all, Abraham was fully persuaded that God had spoke to him and that God was leading him. You must be fully persuaded that God is with you. Secondly, Abraham had seen something, "He had seen a city, with foundations, whose builder and maker is God." I believe that God had given Abraham the same vision that he gave John on the isle of Patmos. John saw the "New Jerusalem coming down from heaven" (Revelations 21).

This vision of Abraham fully dominated his life. He was willing to move out on faith. Thirdly, Abraham's goal was in seeking this country (homeland). His thoughts, his dreams and his desires were with going forward. He was completely over the fact that Ur was in his past. So Abraham pressed ahead believing that God had something much better for him than the City of Ur. If Abrahams' mind and heart would not have been filled with these thoughts and convictions, he would have returned back to Ur when things got rough for him.

Hebrews 11:15, "And truly, if they had been mindful of that country from whence they came out, they might have had opportunity to have returned."

Hebrews 11:15, "If they had been thinking with (homesick) remembrance of that country from which they were emigrants, they would have found constant opportunity to return to it." (Amplified)

Hebrews 11:15, "If they had been thinking of that country that they had left, they would have had opportunity to return." (NIV)

You cannot be consumed with thinking about what you are leaving. Some kinds of thoughts will produce (homesickness). All of us know something about the feeling of homesickness when we left home for the first time. But after the period of homesickness, we settled in knowing that this place was ordained for us at the time. Abraham was able to conquer this homesickness by being filled with the thoughts and conviction that God had something for him much better. Do you believe that God has something for you much better? I believe it because when God promotes us He always promotes us to something better.

Hebrews 11:16, "But now they desire a better country…"

Hebrews 11:16, "Instead, they were longing for a better country…" (NIV)

Hebrews 11:16, "But the truth is that they were yearning for and aspiring to a better and more desirable country…" (Amplified)

We all have seen the images of Haitians on television traveling in boats across the dangerous ocean to come to America. Millions of foreigners yearn to live in America. I have personally traveled and visited in the country of Haiti. It is the most impoverished country in the western hemisphere. When these Haitians get into the boats they know that it is a good chance that they could be drowned by the fierce waves or turned back by the American government. But because they long for a better country and a better quality of life they believe that the risk is worth it all. We must believe that God has something better from what we came out of. I believe it and I praise God for it!

A Faith that Sees Beyond the Natural
Hebrews 11:16 "But now they desire a better
country, that is, a heavenly:"

When you know (convinced) that God has something better for you then you can move forward. Many of us are still trapped into our past with unhealed hurts, damaged emotions and unforgiving hearts. These strongholds will always tie you to the past. But the Lord desires that you move forward. Forward means moving into the future. You can only move forward by releasing the past and asking the Lord to free you through the power of his blood.

Philippians 3:13-14, "Brethren, I count not myself to have apprehended: but this one thing I do, forgetting those things which are behind, and reaching forth unto those things which are before. I press toward the mark of the high calling of God in Christ Jesus."

As you move forward God gives you the insight to see beyond the natural to the spiritual. Many times what is better is not necessarily bigger but better is always spiritual. What Abraham saw was "heavenly".

Hebrews 11:16, "But now they desire a better country, that is, a heavenly…"

What they saw was that which was spiritual! When God opens up our spiritual eyes and spiritual understanding we can see beyond the natural. This spiritual perspective of Abraham's faith walk allowed him not to be tied down to things, people and places. That is why he confessed (he verbally) proclaimed that he was a stranger and a pilgrim on this earth. It didn't bother him to live in a tent because he knew that he was on the move until he reached that city. Let God open your eyes so that you can always see the spiritual side of things. And when you see the (heavenly side) you will also see God at work in His own special and marvelous way.

A Faith that Embraces God
Hebrews 11:16b, "Wherefore God is not ashamed to be called their God: for he hath prepared for them a city."

Our faith must embrace God. Much of the popular Christian teaching concerning faith is faith only in ourselves. That we are the ones that make it happen with our skills and human efforts. But it is faith in God that conquers all. Abraham knew that because of his faith in God that he could embrace God and God would embrace him. What a concept to think about and receive. That because of Jesus Christ that God embraces us and that He is not ashamed to be called our God. Matter of fact, He encourages us to call Him "Abba, Father" which means "Papa, God." It's so good to embrace God as the source of your everything. The old patriarchs believed that beyond this life that God has prepared an eternal city in which the family of God would dwell and be satisfied by Him forever and forever!

Questions & Answers

1) What painful experiences have you endured lately?

_____

_____

_____

_____

2) Have you let go of your past yet?

_____

_____

_____

_____

3) Do you believe that God has something better?

_____

_____

_____

_____

4) What new dreams do you have for the future?

_____

_____

_____

_____

7

Faith Under Trial
Hebrews 11:17-19
Objective: Learning how to victoriously pass the spiritual tests in your life.

By faith Abraham, when he was tried, offered up Isaac: and he that had received the promises offered up his only begotten son. (Hebrews 11: 17)

Introduction

All of us have experienced some educational training from elementary, junior high and high school. Most of us received every six-weeks a report card or some progress report. Those grades were the product of weeks of listening to our teacher, class work, taking notes, homework, study time and testing. The testing although at times we thought was designed to kill us but was in reality given to us as a measure of our comprehension of the materials given to us over a period of time.

But also our testing was designed as a measure of our growth to move from one grade to the next. The goal was for graduation. At graduation we should have acquired the necessary skills and tools to function in the society. As believers in Jesus Christ, God also designs for us tests. These tests are designed that we grow into spiritual maturity and into the likeness of Jesus Christ. Every test gives us the opportunity to experience God in a more meaningful and powerful way. Today we will learn from the life of Abraham, five dynamic principles in passing the tests of faith.

Your Faith Will be Tested
Hebrews 11:17, "By faith Abraham, when he was tried...."

In the life of Abraham he experienced tests over and over again. At seven different points was the character of Abraham tested. First, there was the trying of the fervor of his faith-did he love God more than home and kindred. Secondly, there was the trying of the sufficiency of his faith- was he looking to the living God to supply his need or was he looking at the circumstances around him. Thirdly, there was the trying of the humility of his faith- would he assert his "rights" or yield to Lot? Fourth, there was the trying of the boldness of his faith-would he dare attempt the rescue of his nephew from the hands of a powerful warrior? Fifth, there was the trying of the dignity of his faith-would he take the money and honors from the King of Sodom? Sixth, there was the trying of the patience of his faith-would he wait for God to fulfill His word in His own good time and way, or would he take matters into his own hands and impregnate Hagar his maid.

But now we come to the seventh of the tests in Abraham's life. The most supreme of them all. I want you to know that Abraham did not pass all the spiritual tests in his life. But just as Abraham was tested, you will be tested in all these seven areas. Our faith is tried and tested in order to display its genuineness. A faith that is incapable of enduring trial is no faith at all.

I Peter 1:7, "That the trial of your faith, being much more precious than of gold that perisheth, though it be tried with fire, might be found unto praise and honor and glory at the appearing of Jesus Christ."

You will be Challenged to Surrender Something that you Love with all of Your Heart
Hebrews 11:17, "By faith Abraham, when he was tried, offered up Isaac: and he that had received the promises offered up His only begotten son."

In the Genesis 22 account God spoke to Abraham about offering up his son Isaac. Isaac was the son of promise. Isaac was the miracle child of Abraham and Sarah. They had waited for twenty-five years for God to manifest his promise. The promises of God were all tied to Isaac. Now God is asking Abraham to surrender his son. Can you imagine how much that Abraham loved this child? God knew the deep love between this father and son!

Genesis 22:1-2, "And it came to pass after these things, that God did tempt (test) Abraham, and said unto him, Abraham: and he said, Behold, here I am. And he said, Take now thy son, thine only son Isaac, whom thou lovest, and get thee into the land of Moriah; and offer him there for a burnt offering upon one of the mountains which I will tell thee of."

God was aware of this love but yet he challenged Abraham to surrender that (Isaac) which he loved the most. Usually the test will involve you giving up that which is most precious to your heart. This was not the first time that Abraham had to surrender something that he loved. Up to this time Abraham had surrendered four great things or persons that were the objects of his life. First of all, he had been asked to surrender his home and his kindred. Secondly, he had surrendered His nephew Lot. Third, he had given up his first son, Ishmael. Can you imagine the grief of Abraham when he had to put out Hagar and Ishmael. Ishmael was thirteen years old and was his own flesh and blood. This separation broke his heart. And now God is commanding Abraham not just to separate from Isaac but to kill him, offer him upon an altar as a sacrifice. Haven't you notice lately those things and persons that God is separating you from, especially those who you really love. This is God's method and God's way. He knows what He is doing. Be well aware that when God asks you to surrender what you love that He is bringing you closer to Himself. The word says that Isaac was Abraham's only son and begotten son! Only means that there is not anything left!

Hebrews 11:17, "By faith Abraham….offered up his only begotten son…"

Can you surrender what you are most in love with? Don't be afraid to let it go! God knows how you are struggling with this but be comforted to know He gave up His only begotten son for us a ransom for our sins.

John 3:16, "For God so loved the world that He gave his only begotten Son, that whosoever believeth in him should not perish but have everlasting life."

God will never ask you to do something that He has not done Himself. So through faith and the grace of God you can surrender it, though you love it with all of your heart.

You must Exercise Obedience
Hebrews 11:19, "Accounting that God was able…"

It is interesting that when Abraham heard the voice of God concerning the offering up of Isaac, that he did not hesitate or argue with God. The secret to his obedience was that he had learned to hear the voice of God. He had spent so much time with God that he knew the voice of God. There are so many voices in the world today that the voice of God many times is drowned out. But Abraham over the years had learned to recognize God's voice and trust Him. Abraham heard the voice of God and moved out early the next day to accomplish God's will through obedience.

Genesis 22:3, "And Abraham rose up early in the morning, and saddled his ass, and took two of his young men with him, and Isaac his son, and clave the wood for the burnt offering, and rose up, and went unto the place which God had told him."

Abraham was determined to obey God even though he did not

understand what God was doing. Also, we have no record that he consulted with his wife Sarah. Perhaps if he had consulted with Sarah, she would have discouraged him from doing the will of God. There are times that we must just obey, even when we don't understand it all. Our obedience to God is tied with our love for God. We can't truly say that we love the Lord but are not willing to obey Him. Abraham's love for God was greater than his love for even his son Isaac.

John 14:15, "If ye love me, keep my commandments."

John 14: 21, "He that hath my commandments, and keepeth them, he it is that loveth me: and he that loveth me shall be loved of my Father, and I will love him, and will manifest myself to him."

There is no name –it- and-claim it! You will have to exercise obedience. Obedience is the only way! Now Abraham believed that God was going to do something if he obeyed. Abraham did not pray that God would change His will. Sometimes when we hear God's word or God's direction for our lives, we began to pray that God's will be changed. What we are really doing is asking God to change His agenda so that our agenda may be done. But Abraham didn't question or beg God that Isaac be not offered. He simply obeyed! Now in his obedience he believed that if he killed Isaac that God was able to raise him from the dead.

God will move and you will experience God in a more meaningful and powerful way.

Hebrews 11:19, "Accounting that God was able to raise him up, even from the dead..."

Abraham believed that if he obeyed God, that God was going to provide a resurrection. No one had even heard nothing like this before. That God could raise the dead. Up to this point, God had never manifested His power to raise the dead. But Abraham believed this. Now we are not saying that God told him that! But he believed that this was the only way that God could work this thing out. Isaac was the seed! Isaac was the vessel of bringing forth a nation. But how could God bring forth the seed with a dead Isaac except God raise him from the dead. Sometimes our best thoughts are not God's way! Abraham had a good revelation but it was to be God's way. God was going to move but not as Abraham thought.

Don't get caught up in how God is going to move. Just be confident that God is going to move and that you will experience Him. Abraham thought that Isaac would be slain. Abraham went to the mountain, built the altar and placed Isaac on that altar. But when Abraham raised up the knife to thrust it in the heart of Isaac, God moved.

Genesis 22:10-14, "And Abraham stretched forth his hand, and took the knife to slay his son. And the angel of the Lord called unto him out of heaven, and said, Abraham, Abraham: and he said, Here am I. And he said, Lay not thine hand upon the lad, neither do thou anything unto him: for now I know that thou fearest God, seeing thou hast not withheld thy son, thine only son from me. And Abraham lifted up his eyes, and looked, and behold behind him a ram caught in a thicket by his horns: and Abraham went and took the ram, and offered him up for a burnt offering in the stead of his son. And Abraham called the name of that place Jehovah-Jireh…"

It was never God's intention that Isaac be killed, it was only a test. Could Abraham give up the love of his heart (Isaac) for God? Abraham through this experience and this test would experience God as Jehovah-Jireh (God who is my Provider). The ram would be sacrificed in the stead of Isaac. This was God's plan all along. Though Abraham faith was on trial, he stood fast upon the word and exercised obedience. This is not the end of the story because God spoke again from heaven and pronounced another blessing upon Abraham.

Genesis 22:15-18, "And the angel of the Lord called unto Abraham out of heaven the second time, And said, By myself have I sworn, saith the Lord, for because thou hast done this thing, and hast not withheld thy son, thine only son: That in blessing I will bless thee, and in multiplying I will multiple thy sees as the stars of the heaven, and as the sand which is upon the seashore; And thy seed shall possess the gate of his enemies; And in thy seed shall all the nations of the earth be blessed; because thou hast obeyed my voice."

During the test and after the test is over, you will come to know God in a way that you have never known Him before. God told Abraham, "Now I Know" and "Because you obeyed my voice" that I can truly bless you. I believe that God really wants to bless you, but can He trust you to be obedient to Him no matter what?

Questions & Answers

1) Can you identify the test that you are presently in?

_____

_____

_____

_____

2) What is it that you are struggling with to surrender?

_____

_____

_____

_____

3) Are you exercising obedience in this area?

_____

_____

_____

_____

4) In what area are you experiencing God?

_____

_____

_____

8

Faith and Generational Blessings
Hebrews 11:20-22
Objective: Learning that the blessings of God can be passed down from generation to generation

"And Joseph said unto his father, they are my sons, whom God hath given me in this place. And he said, bring them, I pray thee, unto me and I will bless them." (Genesis 48:9)

Introduction

Usually when a patient sees his or her doctor, there is a long form to be filled with many questions on one's medical history. The medical history includes the medical status of one's parents and siblings. The reason is because there is a direct link from one generation to the next. Also there is a link of the blessings of God from generation to generation. God has said in His word that He is able, "To visit the iniquities of the fathers even to the fourth generation". God can also release His blessings even to the fourth generation.

Many times in the Old Testament God referred to Himself as the "God of Abraham, Isaac and Jacob". He was revealing to us that He is the God who rejoices in blessing families and their children and their children's children. God sees His blessings flowing from one generation to the next. In our lesson we will learn how to be the recipients and channels of the blessings of God. Get ready for an exciting breakthrough in today's lesson.

Profile of Isaac

Strengths and Accomplishments

- The miracle son of Abraham and Sarah
- Married Rebekah
- Father of twin sons Esau and Jacob

Weakness and Mistakes:

- Was very passive
- He loved one son more than he loved his other son

Lessons from His Life:

- As a father he showed favoritism between his children that caused great heartache in his family

Profile of Jacob

Strengthens and Accomplishments:

- Became the father that birthed twelve sons who became the twelve tribes of Israel
- The father of Joseph

Weakness and Mistakes:

- Wanted spiritual things but resorted to carnal schemes
- Stole his brothers' Esau birthright
- Deceived his father Isaac for the blessing

Lessons from His Life:

- Jacob the trickster became Israel the prince when he was broken by God

Profile of Joseph

Strengths and Accomplishments
- Became the prime minister of Egypt
- Saved the world from economic crisis
- Brought his entire family to live with him to Egypt
- Survived slavery and imprisonment

Weakness and Mistakes:
- Walked in pride in his early years as a teenager

Lesson from life
- Although mistreated by his brothers, sold into slavery, falsely accused on a rape charge Joseph operated with the favor of God in his life and prospered.

Acknowledge that God is the Source of All Blessings
Hebrews 11: By faith Isaac blessed...

I grew up in at a time when in preparation for marriage there were at least two things that I knew I needed to secure. First of all, the consent of my girlfriend (now my wife) to agree to marriage and then secure the blessings of her parents. It was never an option to get married without the express blessing of her parents, especially her father. So after, she said "yes" to my marriage proposal then I immediately meet with her parents and asked them for her hand in marriage. After they conferred on us their blessings then we began to plan for a wedding.

Isaac was the miracle son of Abraham and Sarah. Now many years have passed and he is now married with a family of his own. He is the father of two sons, Esau the eldest and Jacob the younger (they are twins). In Jewish culture, the father of the family was the only one that could confer the blessings of the family's inheritance (which included property, money, livestock, etc.) to the children.

Esau the eldest son of Isaac sold his birthright to his brother Jacob for a bowl of soup. But Jacob still had to secure the blessing. Although Jacob used trickery and deceit to secure it, he had a hunger for spiritual things. He used carnal means to secure spiritual things.

So Isaac blessed both Esau and Jacob concerning things to come.

Hebrews 11: 20, "By faith Isaac blessed Jacob and Esau concerning things to come."

Both sons were blessed! Esau became the father of the country of Edom, the people living there called the Edomites. Jacob became the father of twelve sons who became the twelve tribes of Israel through which our Lord Jesus Christ came through. Although Esau was made subservient to Jacob he was still blessed. Do you see how Isaac's blessing flowed down into the future. Therefore the greatest discovery in the life of a human being is that God is the source of blessings. Spiritual blessings are superior to material blessings.

Ephesians 1:3, "Blessed be the God and father of our Lord Jesus Christ who hath blessed us with all spiritual blessings in heavenly places in Christ."

James 1:17, "Every good gift and every perfect gift is from above, and cometh down from the Father of lights."

Acknowledge that it is God that pours to us His blessings every day.

Receiving the Blessings of God through Brokenness
Hebrews 11:21, "By faith Jacob, when he was dying,
blessed both the sons of Joseph; and worshipped,
leaning upon the top of his staff."

This verse says that Jacob was leaning on his staff. Jacob walked with a stick. His staff was always a reminder of his experience of brokenness.

Jacob was self-willed and independent! But one night he received the blessing of God through an encounter with God when God got a hold of him. God finally brought Jacob to the end of himself.

Genesis 32:24-29, "And Jacob was left alone: and there wrestled a man with him until the breaking of the day. And when he saw that he prevailed not against him, he touched the hollow of his thigh: and the hollow of Jacob's thigh was out of joint, as he wrestled with him. And he said, let me go, for the day breaketh. And he said, I will not let you thee go, except thou bless me. And he said unto him, what is thy name? And he said, Jacob. And he said, Thy name shall be no more called Jacob, but Israel: for as a prince hast thou power with God and with men, and hast prevailed and he blessed him there."

For many years after this event, Jacob walked with God limping on his staff. Many times it is in the brokenness of life that our greatest blessings come to us. Just think about it, it was in those times of sufferings that you were able to draw closest to the Lord.

II Corinthians 10:9-10, "And he said unto me, My grace is sufficient for thee: for my strength is made perfect in weakness. Most gladly therefore will I rather glory in my infirmities, that power of Christ may rest upon me for when I am weak, then am I strong."

Faith that Becomes a Channel of the Blessings to Others
Hebrews 11:21, "By faith Jacob, when he was dying
blessed both the sons of Joseph; and worshipped…"

God blesses us not that we become containers but that we become channels of those blessings. He blesses us so that we might bless others. Joseph being sold into slavery was divine providence. Joseph was put in Egypt so that he might be a preserver for the world. When famine hit the land of Canaan, God moved Jacob and his entire family to Egypt where they were all reconciled and restored back into fellowship with Joseph. Even on Jacob's death bed, he worshipped God and spoke blessings into the life of his two grandsons. You and I must learn how to speak blessings in the lives of others.

Genesis 48: 20-21, "And he blessed them that day, saying… God shall be with thee."

God used Jacob to speak through the gift of the word of knowledge, the word of wisdom and prophecy into his heirs concerning the promises of God. Today when we learn to continue to yield to the Holy Spirit, God desires that we be used to speak His word. Jacob never thought that he would see Joseph alive but God blessed him to see Joseph's children. It is such a blessing in itself to have people (family, friends) in which we can encourage. Speak blessings not curses into people's life and also your own life. Don't curse your blessings by always speaking negative words but learn to speak forth faith words. Always remember that life and death is in the power of the tongue. Use words to empower and inspire yourself and others. By doing so you are becoming a channel of blessings.

Questions & Answers

1) What generational blessings are in your family?

_____

_____

_____

_____

2) What blessings do you hope are imparted to your children?

_____

_____

_____

_____

3) Have you been broken by God?

_____

_____

_____

_____

4) How will you be a channel for blessings to others?

_____

_____

_____

_____

9

The Faith of a Champion
Hebrews 11:23-29
Objective: Learning how to make good decisions that causes us to victoriously walk in our assignment.

By faith Moses, when he was come to years, refused to be called the son of Pharaoh's daughter; choosing rather to suffer affliction with the people of God, than to enjoy the pleasures of sin for a season. (Hebrews 11:24-25)

Introduction

One of the greatest scientific champion's ever produced in this nation was an African- American named George Washington Carver. He was a genius scientist that produced over three hundred products from a peanut. His discoveries helped to bless the entire world. He worked at Tuskegee Institute in Alabama with Booker T. Washington. One day he was approached by a committee from a much larger and prestige white university. They offered him a greater financial package if he would only leave Tuskegee and come and transfer to their university.

This offer would have afforded him much more financial security for his family and perhaps much more national and international recognition. But George Washington Carver refused their offer and made a decision to remain at Tuskegee. He said, "Tuskegee is my true assignment on this earth." Dr. Carter chose to remain with his people (African –Americans) that he might help to lift them up.

We as believers in Jesus Christ have the opportunity to make decisions that will help us to become "Champions for God." In today's lesson we will learn how to utilize our faith that will empower us to overcome fear. The fear of failure is perhaps the greatest hindrance in moving out into the great things of God. But through faith we have the power to overcome those things that seem to be impossible. Life is really a series of choices. One poet has said, "It is not in life's chances but rather in life's choices that happiness will come." Moses chose a life of service to his suffering people over a life of becoming perhaps the next King in Egypt. You can choose to become a Champion for God today?

Profile of Moses

Strengths and Accomplishments

- Became the Great Emancipator of the Nation of Israel from slavery
- Served as Israel's Leader for forty-years
- Lived in Egypt as a Prince for forty-years
- Lived in the desert of Midian as a shepherd for forty-years
- Educated and trained as a military general in Egypt
- Adopted son of Pharaoh's daughter
- Talked with God face to face
- Was the instrument of great miracles

Weakness and mistakes

- Moses moved out before time and murdered a man
- Moses impatience prohibited him from going into the Promised Land.

Lessons from his life

- God calls and preserves His servants and empowers them for service.

- Our greatest weakness can become our greatest strength when placed in the hands of the Lord

The Devil Wants to Kill You
Hebrews 11:23, "By faith Moses, when he was born, was hid three months of his parents, because they saw he was a proper child…"

The word of God makes it plain in John 10:10 that the enemy comes to, "Kill, Steal and Destroy." The enemy if he could have would have killed you a long time ago. But God has preserved you for a divine and unique purpose. In the time of our text the Children of Israel has been in slavery in the land of Egypt for over four hundred years. Those years in Egypt were years of great affliction and suffering. The more that the children of Israel were afflicted, the more that they grew and multiplied. And the people of Egypt became afraid that the children of Israel would grow to overpower and overthrow them. So Pharaoh made a decree that all of the male babies born would be killed. The enemy wants to kill you.

Exodus 1: 8-14, "Now there arose up a new king over Egypt, which knew not Joseph. And he said unto his people, Behold, the people of the children of Israel are more and mightier than we: Come on, let us deal wisely with them; lest they multiply, and it come to pass, that, when there falleth out any war, they join also unto our enemies, and fight against us, and so get them up out of the land. Therefore they did set over them taskmasters to afflict them with their burdens. But the more they afflicted them, the more they multiplied and grew. And the Egyptians made the children of Israel to serve with rigour: And they made their lives bitter. And the King of Egypt spake to the Hebrew midwives and said, when ye do the office of a midwife to the Hebrew women, and see them upon the stools; if it be a son, then ye shall kill him: but if it be a daughter, then she shall live."

The enemy wanted to kill the baby boys. Doesn't that sound familiar to our day. The "genocide" to destroy the males in our society. Now the devil is not just after the males but he wants to destroy the females as well. The devil wants to kill you. Don't you know by virtue that you are here today proves that the devil was not successful. All of the things that he has been throwing in your path has just made you stronger. You must be aware that you are in a spiritual warfare.

Ephesians 6: 12, "For we wrestle not against flesh and blood, but against principalities, against powers, against the rulers of the darkness of this world, against spiritual wickedness in high places."

A Faith that Overcomes Fear
Hebrews 11:23, "By faith Moses, when he was born, was hid
three months of his parents, because he was a proper child;
and they were not afraid of the king's commandment."

If you are going to be powerful in God, you will have to learn to overcome fear. Fear is one of the most potent weapons of the enemy. We are fearful of many things: flying, giving, relationships, change, people etc. But your faith must be greater than your fears. When the king gave the command that the new born baby boys be killed; there were two group of people that did not succumb to the fear of the king. First of all the midwives feared God more than they did the king. Your fear of God (reverence) must be stronger all other fears in your life.

Exodus 1:17, "But the midwives feared God, and did not as the king of Egypt commanded them, but saved the men children alive?"

The midwives were more committed to doing the will of God than they were in obeying the voice of the king. They were not worried about the threats of what the king would do to them. They believed that they were in the hands of the Lord. The scripture says, "That the Lord dealt with the midwives." I believe that the Lord imparted supernatural strength and courage in the hearts of these midwives.

God will impart and give His supernatural strength and courage in the face of your fears.

Isaiah 40: 29, "He giveth power to the faint (weak); and to them that have no might (strength) he increaseth strength."

When the king saw that the midwives were not going to kill the new born baby boys right out of the womb, then he order that the new born baby boys be cast into the Nile River. If you stand up to the devil he will change his strategy. But there was somebody else that would not be ruled by fear in their lives. A husband by the name of Amram and his wife Jochbed

I Timothy 1: 7, "God hast not given us the spirit of fear..."

How many times in your life have you made a decision out of fear. This husband and wife would make a little basket (water proof) and place the basket in the Nile under the care of the Lord. While the little basket floated in the river God sent the king's daughter to bathe. It was a divine meeting. The princess took the little child to the palace with her and Moses grew up in royalty by the Egyptians. God's preserving power was at work. All because Moses parents refused to be governed by the emotion of fear. They choice to put their little baby in the Nile River by faith.

Hebrews 11:23, "They (Amram and Jocebed) were not afraid of the king's commandments."

Don't let fear ever again rule you! Let the faith of God explode within your heart.

Accepting your Assignment
Hebrews 11: 24-25 By faith Moses, when he was come

*to years, refused to be called the son of Pharaoh's
daughter; Choosing rather to suffer with the people of
God, than to enjoy the pleasures of sin for a season.*

While growing up in the palace Moses was exposed to the best
in education, wealth, training, religion that the world could offer.
Although he was an adopted prince, his heart went out for the
Israelites. He saw the cruel treatment as slaves and he identified
with them. Somewhere perhaps he was introduced to his biological
mother, father, brother and sister. Rather than running away from
who he was, he made a conscious decision that he was going to deliver
his people.

So at the age for forty years old he stepped out to do so but
he was not yet prepared. He murdered a man. I believe that at
forty years of old age he decided to refuse to be called the son of
Pharaoh's daughter. He forsakes all that his culture had to offer
even to the point of perhaps his sitting on the throne one day.
Moses accepted his assignment as a deliver. All of us have been
given an assignment on this earth to solve some problem.

- A dentist solves tooth problems.
- A mechanic solves car problems
- A lawyer solves legal problems
- A minister solves spiritual problems
- A mother solves a child's problem
- A teacher solves an education problem

You have an assignment to solve some problem. You will leave a
legacy by the problem that you solve on this earth. Moses chose the
pathway of suffering affliction. Very few of us are inclined to live a
life of suffering. But Moses choose that life. He consciously choose
to suffer rather than enjoy the pleasures of sin for a season.

The phrase "pleasures of sin for a season" is all the wealth,
fame, power and prestige that went along with him being the son
of Pharaoh's daughter. He literally rejected the lifestyle of the rich

and famous to become a servant to the people of God. Talking about a great champion. To him justice, righteousness and freedom of a people was more important than him sitting upon the throne of all of Egypt!

Walking in True Riches
Hebrews 11: 26, "Esteeming the reproach of Christ greater riches than the treasures in Egypt: for he had respect unto the recompense of the reward."

Moses found the secret of joy and contentment in his life. He found what were the true riches of life. His inner being was not filled with the substitutes that many of us are in search of. He found that in God he could experience true satisfaction. Egypt had great riches and he could have lived a life in these riches but he found something greater. Moses found a cause by which he could live. Even die for.

God gave him revelation that suffering the reproaches of Christ was better than great riches. Moses found out that he could communicate with God face to face. He could talk with God! He could be used as a vessel of God to perform miracles! He could teach the people the statues of God!

This was more important to Him. God is desiring that you find for yourself this kind of satisfaction. Also Moses could see the reward in what he was doing. Do you realize that what we do for Christ will last! Preaching, teaching and ministering has eternal impact. Moses had respect for that reward. Even though he was leading the people to a promised land on earth, he had the wisdom to know that God was doing far more than giving the people real estate. Walk in the true riches and become a champion for God.

Questions & Answers

1) When did the devil try to kill you?

_____

_____

_____

_____

2) Identify the fear factor in you life?

_____

_____

_____

_____

3) How are you using your faith to overcome fear?

_____

_____

_____

_____

4) What true riches have you discovered in your life?

_____

_____

_____

_____

10

Faith's Marching Orders for Victory
Hebrews 11:30-31
Objective: Learning how to use our
faith in spiritual warfare.

By faith the walls of Jericho fell down, after they were compassed about seven days. (Hebrews 11:30)

Introduction

Even though the children of Israel entered into the Promised Land, they still had to conquer cities. They had to advance by learning how to fight the enemy. The life of faith is a life of battles as well as blessings. As we make advancements into our true inheritance in Christ, the enemy tries to attack us and tries to discourage and defeat us. This explains why the word says, "Be strong and courageous." Where can we get the strength and courage that we need to face the enemy and claim the victory?

We can get these blessings only as we trust God's word. It is here that Israel's conquest of Jericho becomes an object lesson of the victory that comes through faith. You and I can overcome the enemy and claim the inheritance in the same way that Joshua conquered Jericho. Because God had brought the children of Israel to this place, He had a plan to take the city! Let us learn how to seek God for His strategies and plans for our lives.

Today we will learn how to walk corporately in spiritual warfare and spiritual victory. As we learn how to move together in the things of God, we will experience more joy and peace.

71

Profile of Joshua

Strengthens and Accomplishments

- Moses' assistant and successor
- One of only two adults who experienced Egyptian slavery and lived to enter the promised land
- Led the Israelites into their God-given homeland
- Brilliant military strategist
- Faithful to ask God's direction in the challenges he faced

Lessons from his life:

- Effective leadership is often the product of good preparation and encouragement
- The persons after whom we pattern ourselves will have a definite effect on us
- A person committed to God provides the best model for us

The Enemy is Already Defeated
Hebrews 11:30, "By faith…"

The city of Jericho was impregnable. There were no human means available to defeat it. But Joshua knew that since, God had brought him and the people into this new land, that God indeed had a plan for defeating the enemy and taking the city of Jericho. Just before the battle, Joshua went out to survey the situation, and suddenly he met a stranger.

Joshua 5:13-15 Now it came about when Joshua was by Jericho, that he lifted up his eyes and looked, and behold, a man was standing opposite him with his sword drawn in hand, and Joshua went to him and said to him, "Are you for us or our adversaries?" And he said, "No rather I indeed come now as captain of the host of the Lord." And Joshua fell on his face to the earth, and bowed down, and said to him, "What has my Lord to say to his servant?" And

the captain of the Lord's host said to Joshua, "Remove your sandals from your feet, for the place where you are standing is holy." And Joshua did so.

It was Jesus Christ that Joshua met (Sometimes Jesus revealed himself in the Old Testament in different forms. This is called theophany), and that meeting was the assurance of victory. Jesus showed up as the Military General! Public victories are the outcome of private meetings with the Lord. When Joshua faced Jericho, he knew he was not alone: the Lord was with him. Furthermore, he discovered that he was second in command! All he had to do was take orders from the Lord and the victory was secure. "See," said the Lord, "I have given Jericho into your hand..." (Joshua 6:2). God said to Joshua, "I want you to see, it has already been done." "See" was a definite call to view things with the eye of the spirit rather than that of the body: contemplate this obstacle by faith and not with carnal reason. He had already won the victory! All Joshua had to do was follow orders and, by faith, claim the city for God. Satan has already been defeated at Calvary but we must secure directions from God daily.

God has the Strategy for Every Victory
Hebrews 11:30, 'By faith the walls of Jericho....'

One of the most important elements of walking with God is realizing that we must seek God for directions. God has the plan and strategy for every victory in our lives. This is vital in the corporate relationship of the church. God has a specific plan for his church and also for every individual or local body. The leader (Pastor) must seek God for His instructions concerning the direction of the church. One of our greatest problems has been the attempt to walk in self-sufficiency, trying to lead in our own strength and with our limited wisdom. Also another problem has been the misconception of church boards in the government of the church. A church board is secular concept that has been adopted by the body of Christ.

It has been God's design through out all of the scriptures that His church be led by His consecrated leadership. But the Pastor must be a man who daily seeks God for His directions. Joshua sought God for the strategy for taking Jericho.

Had Joshua called a council of war and consulted with the heads of the tribes as to what they deemed the best policy to adopt, what conflicting advice, he had most probably received what various methods of assault had been advocated. One would have reasoned that the only way to subdue Jericho was by starving out of its inhabitants through a protracted siege. Another would have counseled the use of ladders to scale its walls by men heavy armed. A third would have argued that heavy battering-rams would be most effective. While a fourth would have suggested a surprise attack by secretly tunneling under the walls. Each would have leaned unto his own understanding, and deemed his plan the best. But Joshua conferred not with flesh and blood, but received his commission direct from the Lord, and therein he has left an example for all His servants to follow. The minister of the Gospel is responsible to Christ: he is the servant, called and commissioned by Him, and from Him alone must he take orders. He has no authority except what Christ has given him, and he needs no more. Joshua did not refer the instructions he received from God to the judgment of the priests and elders and ask their opinion on the same, but instead acted promptly upon them, counting upon the divine blessing, however his fellows might regard them.

God desires to give us the orders! If we would but seek His face concerning all matters, then we would get the strategy for our victory.

Jeremiah 29:11, "For I know the plans that I have for you, says the Lord, plans for your welfare and not your harm, to give you a future with hope." (New Revised Standard Version)

The Leader and the People Must Obey the Orders
Hebrews 11:30," By faith the walls of Jericho fell down,
after they were compassed about seven days."

The orders that Joshua received from God seemed very foolish; but it was still the plans of God. They were to march around the city of Jericho in silence once a day for six days. Then they were to march on the seventh day, seven times. Can you imagine the doubters! God didn't say that! God would not only speak to Joshua in this matter. Nobody is going to tell me when to be silent.

Many times we say these things because in our hearts there is a spirit of rebellion. For some reason, many believers don't like taking orders in the church. They take orders on the job, they take orders in the community and they even talk orders from strangers that they don't even know. But when it comes down to the church and spiritual matters they rebel. God desires that you be obedient! Develop an obedient attitude.

Also develop patience! Faith is not in a hurry, and faith is not worried when people say, "That's foolish!" God still chooses the foolish things of this world to shame and confound the wise (**I Corinthians 1:26-29**). He used Moses' rod, and the priest's trumpets, and David's sling, and a little boy's lunch. He even used a Roman cross! God's methods and tools may seem foolish, but faith in God is not foolish. While the wise men of the world are shaking their heads in disbelief, the children of God are lifting their hearts in joyful faith and watching God do miracles.

The victory of Jericho was not the result of "great faith" so much as faith in a great God. The next time, in the will of God, you face a Jericho situation in your life, pause to find out what God's battle plan is, and dare to believe it and obey it. What He asks you to do may seem foolish, but that is where faith comes in. Faith is not believing in spite of evidence; it is obeying in spite of circumstance or consequence.

"In the world you have tribulations," our Lord said to His disciples, "but take courage, I have overcome the world" (John 16:33). The world system around us builds high its Jericho's and dares us to attack them; but the believer knows that every stronghold of the enemy has already been defeated at the Cross. We do not fight for victory; we fight from victory to victory.

On that seventh day the priests blew the trumpets, they shouted and the walls came down. With obeying the orders the walls will come down. We can shout because the victory is ours.

Joshua 6:20, "When the trumpets sounded, the people shouted, and at the sound of the trumpet, when the people gave a loud shout, the wall collapsed; so every man charged straight in, and took the city." (NIV)

Questions & Answers

1) Do you know the strategy to your battle?

_____

_____

_____

_____

2) What are you battling against right now?

_____

_____

_____

_____

3) What instructions have been placed before you?

_____

_____

_____

_____

4) What areas do you need courage to defeat the enemy?

_____

_____

_____

_____

11

Rahab's Faith
Hebrews 11:31
Objective: Learning how to be spiritually discerning and taking divine risks for the Lord

By faith the harlot Rahab perished not with them that believed not, when she had received the spies with peace. (Hebrews 11:31)

Introduction

It is amazing how God is able to save! A preacher once proclaimed, "God is able to save from the gutter most to the uttermost." No human being is out of His reach to rescue and save. In our lesson today, God reaches out to a prostitute! Although she had used her body as a vessel of dishonor for many years, although she jumped from bed to bed and slept with countless men, although she lived a life of humiliation and shame, she broke through her past and gave her heart to the Lord.

God forgave her, transformed her and saved her from destruction. She was brought into the congregation of the Israelite people. She became the mother of Boaz and the great grandmother of King David. It would be through her lineage that our Lord Jesus Christ would come. Today we will look into Rahab's faith. By modeling her faith we can become persons of conviction who dare to obey God and do His will.

Profile of Rahab

Strengthens and Accomplishments

- Rahab was a survivor
- Married Salmon an Israelite even though she was a Canaanite
- Mother of Boaz
- Great grandmother of King David
- Willing to help others at a great cost to herself
- One of only two women mentioned in the Hall of Faith

Weakness and Mistake

- She was a prostitute

Lessons Learned from Her Life

- We must not gauge a person's interest in God by their background or appearance.
- She did not let fear affect her faith in a God that she didn't even know.
- God often uses people of simple faith to accomplish his great purposes, no matter what past they have had or how insignificant they seem to be.
- Rahab didn't allow her past to keep her from her new role God had for her.

Key Verses:

- Rahab's story is told in Joshua 2 and 6.
- She is also mentioned in Matthew 1:5; Hebrews 11:31; and James 2:25.

Everybody Has a Past
Hebrews 11:31, "By faith the harlot Rahab..."

It was time for Joshua and the children of Israel to cross over the

Jordan River and take into possession the city of Jericho. Joshua decides to sent two spies to view the city and come back and make the report to him. There is something very important when God gets ready to do a job. He works on both sides of the line. On one side God is going to use two Israelite spies (that is one side of the line) but also there in the city of Jericho (in the enemy camp) God has prepared a citizen of Jericho. The person that God has touched would seem an unlikely candidate. Her name is Rahab! She is a prostitute. God can use anybody that He chooses to use. Your background does not have to be a hindrance to you.

I spoke to a brother who wanted to be used by God but he said, "Every time I try to witness people keep bringing up my past." I smiled and said to him, "That's great!" He looked at me astonished, I continued, "Because all you need to lead someone to Christ is tell them two stories. First of all tell them your story and secondly tell them Jesus' story." He smiled and I continued, "Your past now is not a negative but it is a positive since Jesus has come into your life." Everybody has a past! Rahab was a prostitute who gave her heart to God. And God saved her by His grace. Use your past as a demonstration of the miracle power of God that saved you!

While God had worked on Rahab's heart He was working on the two spies. The two spies needed somewhere to go as they went into Jericho to spy out the enemy camp. Guess where the Holy Spirit led these two spies? You are right! He led them to Rahab's house. When they came knocking she was ready to receive them. While God was working on one end of the line with Joshua and the two spies, He was also at the very same time working on the heart of Rahab even though she had a past. What a marvelous God that we serve. Right now God is working on the other line in your life. He knows what you need and He knows who to touch to help open the door for your miracle.

Faith Comes by Hearing
Hebrews 11:31, "By faith the harlot Rahab perished not with them that believed not..."

When the spies came knocking on her door to find refuge from the Jericho policemen, Rahab received these two spies into her home. Something had happen within her! The faith of God was burning within her heart. She believed that these men were of God and that God had given the Israelites the land. She said, "I know." She was confident that God was with these people and she wanted to be part of what God was doing.

Joshua 2:9, "And she said unto the men, I know that the Lord hath given you the land, and that your terror is fallen upon us, and that all the inhabitants of the land faint because of you."

Rahab believed to the point that she knew that God had already given these people the victory over Jericho. She also recognized that the people of Jericho were afraid of the Israelites. Sometimes people are afraid of you because they see that God is with you. Other times people give you trouble because when you walk in they also know that there is something special about you. Rahab described as "Terror." You see she had heard that how God forty years ago had crossed the children of Israel across the Red Sea! They had heard about the victorious battles that God had given the Israel again the enemies. And that caused even their hearts to melt.

Joshua 2:10, "For we heard how the Lord dried up the water of the Red Sea for you, when ye came out of Egypt; and what ye did unto the two kings of the Amorities, that were on the other side of Jordan, Sihon and Og, whom ye utterly destroyed."

Joshua 2:11, "And as soon as we had heard these things, our hearts did melt, neither did there remain any more courage in any man, because of you: for the Lord your God, he is God in heaven above, and in earth beneath.

Rahab was familiar with Israel's story! The enemy is familiar with your story and he knows that it was the Lord's doing. Notice that

Rahab attributed Israel's victories by the Lord's power. When God brings you out, people will know it and they will recognize that it was God. Rahab believed this history while the other citizens of Jericho did not. Everybody in Jericho was aware of this history. But only Rahab believed it. So when the two spies came to her house she received them in faith. She expressed kindness to them and hid them in her roof.

Joshua 2: 12, "I have shewed you kindness…"

The Discernment of the Believer
Hebrews 11:31, "By faith the harlot Rahab perished not with them that believed not, when she had received the spies with peace."

Rahab received these two spies by faith. There are three things that Rahab discerned about these two spies. First of all she discerned that these two spies were of God. She knew that without a shadow of doubt. Secondly, she knew that God had given them the land. She actually told them so! Thirdly, she knew that they were in danger of being caught by the Jericho soldiers. That is why she hid them in the roof and denied that they were still in her house when the policemen came. How did she know all of this? Because she operated in spiritual discernment! It is necessary in the times that we live in that we also have spiritual discernment. The enemy is a lair and a deceiver!

Ephesians 1:18, "The eyes of your understanding being enlightened."

You need spiritual understanding. Rahab spiritual eyes had been opened up to these spiritual realities. She also discerned that she and her house could be saved. And so she guided the policemen to a wild goose chase.

Joshua 2:4-6, "She said, there came men unto me, but I know not where they went. And it came to pass about the time of the shutting

of the gate, when it was dark, that the men went out: where the men went I don't know: pursue after them quickly: for you shall overtake them. And the men pursued after them the way to Jordan..."

The Language of the Believer
Hebrews 11:31, "....received the spies with peace."

When the two spies came down from the roof after the policemen were gone, Rahab began to talk faith talk. She began to share with the two spies that since she had showed kindness that they should show kindness to her and her family. Rahab wanted to be saved. She asked these two spies to enter into covenant relationship with her.

We need to speak the language as covenant people. She was not afraid to boldly ask to be saved from death. She spoke with so much faith that the men agreed that she and her whole house would be saved.

Joshua 2:12-13, "Now therefore, I pray you, swear unto me by the Lord, since I have shewed you kindness, that ye will also shew kindness unto my father's house, and give me a true token: And that ye will save alive my father, and my mother, and my brethren, and my sisters, and all that they have, and deliver our lives from death."

They all entered into covenant relationship with one another.

The Preservation Power of God

The men were let down off the wall with a rope. But before they left, Rahab gave to them vital instructions. She pointed them to a specific mountain and told them to remain three days. And after three days the course would be clear for them to return back to Joshua. The two spies also gave Rahab vital instructions. She was to get all of her family and put a scarlet rope in the window.

Everything would be destroyed in Jericho except all in the house with the scarlet rope in the window. God was going to reward Rahab's faith and her obedience. And when the Israelites did march around the walls, they came down. All was destroyed except Rahab and her family.

Rahab was preserved by the power of God. She and her entire house were saved. Rahab went with the Israelites and married into the Jewish line. Her marriage gave birth to a great grandson named David. David became the king of Israel. Through this same blood line our Lord Jesus Christ would come. God looked beyond her past into her future. Because of the Almighty God her future was greater than her past. Thank God for the faith of Rahab!

Questions & Answers

1) Identify God's grace in your life?

_____

_____

_____

_____

2) What report have you received?

_____

_____

_____

_____

3) Are you growing in discernment?

_____

_____

_____

_____

4) How have you experienced God's preserving power in your life?

_____

_____

_____

_____

12

A Faith That Inspires Courage
Hebrews 11: 32-40
Objective: Learning to stand against all odds with the divine courage of God!

(Of whom the world was not worthy) Hebrews 11:38

Introduction

We owe so much to the biblical saints. They paid an awesome price for their faith. They endured great obstacles and stood against seemingly impossible odds. Many of them even died for what they believed in. Man's estimate of these heroes of faith was a low one, so men persecuted them, arrested them, tortured them, and in some cases, killed them. But God's estimate is entirely different. He said that the world was not worthy of these people. Today we give thanks for these saints of old, for they were faithful during difficult times, and yet we are the ones who have received the "better blessings." We enjoy them today through Jesus Christ. If the saints of old had not trusted God and obeyed His will, Israel would have perished and the Messiah would not have been born.

The common thread that runs throughout all of their lives was that they had a faith that inspired courage. I call it "moral courage." Oh, how we need this "moral courage" today. I believe that God desires to develop this "courage" within you. With this courage you can stand against everything that seems to be impossible. With this courage we can endure challenges that will only make us stronger in the Lord.

God Uses a Variety of Persons
Hebrews 11:32, "And what shall I more say? For the time would fail me to tell of Gideon and of Barak, and of Samson, and of Jephthae; of David also, and Samuel, and of the prophets:"

As we read this passage, we discover quite a mixture of different kinds of people. There are both men and women, young and old. There are "official people" (kings and prophets) and common people, such as you and me. Some of these were "high born," while others had no special pedigree. I see in this list farmers, shepherds, soldiers, priests, and even the son of a prostitute who grew up as a gang member (Jephthah).

What brought these people together? Faith. We all have a different heredity, different tastes and interests, different skills. Faith doesn't depend on your IQ or physical or psychological equipment; nor does faith depend upon your circumstances. God will honor your faith. In "**Hebrews 11:32**," the writer mentions three periods in Israel's history: the Judges (Gideon, Barak, Samson & Jephthah), the Kings (David), and the Prophets (Samuel). Faith is not limited to one period in history or even one kind of political system. We must not say that faith cannot operate because of the "times" or "circumstances." Because true faith is not limited by history.

Each one of these heroes were just like you and me! They had their weakness, their issues, their problems and their trails. But they cultivated courage to believe God in spite of themselves.

I Corinthians 1:26-28, "For ye see your calling, brethren, how that not many wise men after the flesh, not many mighty, not many noble, are called. But God hath chosen the foolish things of the world to confound the wise; and God hath chosen the weak things of the world to confound the things which are mighty; And base things of the world, and things which are despised, hath God chosen, yea, and things which are not, to bring to nought things that are: That no flesh shall glory in his presence."

God will use anybody who will surrender their will unto him. Our God does not only see us where we are right now but He also sees us in our fullest potential in Him. All of these heroes in (Verse 32) had weaknesses in their lives. Gideon was really a coward when God called him! Barak was a military man that would not go into battle without Deborah, the prophetess by his side. Samson had a problem with lust and the enemy stole his power and eyes. Jephthane was called a "vain fellow" because really he was a gang leader. David committed adultery and murdered a man to try to cover up his sin. Samuel had deep issues with feeling accepted by people. But in spite of these weaknesses these heroes learned that confession, repentance and faith in God was the answer. Each of these heroes made great contributions in the kingdom of God. You can press through your weakness and allow the Lord to strengthen you to do his will. God wants to use you.

You Need "Moral Courage"
Hebrews 11: 33-37 Who through faith subdued kingdoms, wrought righteousness, obtained promises, stopped the mouths of lions, quenched the violence of fire, escaped the edge of the sword, out of weakness were made strong, waxed valiant in fight, turned to flight the armies of the aliens, women received their dead raised to life again: and others were tortured, not accepting deliverance; that they might obtain a better resurrection: And others had trial of cruel mockings and scourgings, yea, moreover of bonds and imprisonment: They were stoned, they were sawn asunder, were tempted, were slain with the sword: they wandered about in sheepskins and goatskins; being destitute, afflicted, and tormented.

There are twenty-one statements made concerning the achievements of faith in **(verses 33-38)**. These are arranged in three groups.

The first group marks **attainments**-the conquering of kingdoms, the establishment of justice, the inheriting of spiritual promises. Verse 33 says that they, **"subdued kingdoms, wrought righteousness**

and obtained promises." What they did as people of God (weaker forces according to the world) overcame the enemies of Israel. They enforced justice in the sense as making it the working principle of the society. These men of faith were "courageous" to choose justice and hate injustice. And because they took this stand, they conquered the kingdoms of the world.

The second group marks special kinds of **deliverances**. These heroes of faith had great deliverances: **(Hebrews 11:33-34)**

"Stopped the mouths of lions…"
"Quenched the violence of fire…"
"Escaped the edge of the sword…"

These people of faith faced lion dens, fiery fire furnaces and even escaped from battles. They were confident, bold and courageous to stand for what they believed. They had a belief system that allowed them to go into some impossible situations. You and I must have a belief system that we should be willing to die for! When they got into trouble God delivered them. He is able to deliver you when you stand up with a **"moral conviction."**

The third group marks special kinds of **endurances.** Because of their **"moral courage"** they endured. They were not delivered out of every situation but they endured many things. When you operate in courage God will give you the strength to endure hardships.

II Timothy 2:3, "Thou therefore endure hardness as a good soldier of Jesus Christ."

God is not going to let you escape all tests in your life. But He will allow you to go through some things that He can develop in you character. These heroes:

"Waxed valiant in fight"…
"Turned to flight the armies of the aliens"…
"Women received their dead raised to life again"…

"Others were tortured, not accepting deliverance; that they might obtain a better resurrection"…
"Others had trial of cruel mockings and scourgings"…
"Moreover of bonds and imprisonment"…
"They were stoned"…
"They were sawn asunder"…
"Were tempted"…
"They wandered about in sheepskins and goatskins"…

"Being destitute"…

"Afflicted"…
"Tormented"…
"They wandered in deserts, and in mountains, and in dens and caves of the earth"…

In Your Weakness God Will Make You Strong
Hebrews11: 34,"…out of weakness were made strong, waxed valiant in fight, turned to flight the armies of the aliens."

These phrases go together as they describe the **"warfare of faith."** We make the mistake of thinking that the great men and women of faith were somehow essentially different from us, but they were not. "All God's giants have been weak men," said J. Hudson Taylor, "who did great things for God because they reckoned on His being with them." The difference is faith! "Want of trust is at the root of almost all our sins and all our weaknesses," said Hudson Taylor.

Apart from the power of God, Samson was as weak as any other man. Gideon was a trembling farmer, hiding in a winepress, when God called him; yet his faith in God made him a conqueror. Barak begged Deborah to assist him in battle, and out of fear and weakness God gave strength and victory. Jephthah was the rejected son of a prostitute, yet God used him to win a mighty victory. God did not substitute strength for their weakness; out of their weakness, He made them strong.

II Corinthians 12:10, "When I am weak, then am I strong."

God made these believers "mighty in war", not mighty before the war. They had the faith to get into the battle; and in the midst of the fight, they were strengthen by the Lord. He gave them the power of His spirit. God will make you strong even in your weakness. He will give you courage. Receive that courage right now! You have the resources of the mighty Holy Spirit available to you for the asking.

You Can Be Better
Hebrews 11: 39-40, "And these all, having obtained a
good report through faith, received not the promise.
God having provided some better thing for us, that
they without us should not be made perfect."

These heroes of faith believed in God. They stood against entire kingdoms, they attained remarkable "the promise." They received many promises from God. It was the promises of God that gave them the inner strength to stand against all odds. But they did not receive the promise (Jesus Christ). You and I have received Jesus.

We should be better, we should be more powerful and certainly we should be more courageous in the face of our challenges. God has given everything that we need to be a success in Him. Therefore grow in faith and maturity so that you can stand against the wiles of the devil. Stand up! Stand up and be counted. Be courageous and never ever give up. There are untapped resources within you ready to be released, if you will only yield to God and trust His word! Unbelief will always lock up your potential, but faith in God will release it.

(Philippians 4:13) "I can do all things through Christ that strengthens me."

Joshua 1: 6-8, "Be strong and of a good courage, only be strong and very courageous, that thou mayest observe to do according to all the law: turn not from it to the right hand or the left, that thou

mayest prosper wither-soever thou goest. This book of the law shall not depart out of thy mouth; but thou shall meditate therein day and night, that thou mayest observe to do according to all that is written therein: for then thou shall make thy way prosperous, and then thou shalt have good success."

Questions & Answers

1) How are you developing "moral courage"?

_____

_____

_____

_____

2) How is God turning your weakness into strengths?

_____

_____

_____

_____

3) What area of warfare do you need victory?

_____

_____

_____

_____

4) How can you be better in your growth?

_____

_____

_____

_____

13

Faith for Mental Toughness
Hebrews 12:3-4
Objective: Learning to fill your
mind with faith thoughts

For consider him that endured such contradiction of sinners against himself, lest ye be wearied and faint in your minds. Ye have not yet resisted unto blood, striving against sin. (Hebrews 12:3-4)

Introduction

Mel Gibson's movie, "The Passion of Christ" struck a tremendous cord with all of us because he portrayed a suffering Christ. The violence that he portrayed that Jesus went through really made many of us cry with shame about our own suffering. Sometimes we think that we are the only one that is going through! Other times we believe that our problems are the only problems.

This causes us to get trapped with a spirit of selfishness! To become self-absorbed with pity! These believers had become self-absorbed with their suffering. Many of them had made decisions to quit their faith in Christ. Others had gone back to the old system of Judaism. But the writer encouraged them to on with Christ and to never give up. God has a greater purpose for our suffering or discipline. He is producing the peaceful fruit of righteous within us.

In today's lesson we are going to learn how to fill our minds and hearts with the "God-Kind" of thoughts. We will be challenged to live above feeling sorry for ourselves to standing up victoriously under any load. God desires to make you tough minded and yet tenderhearted. Let us draw from the strength of today's lesson.

Jesus Endured
Hebrews 12:3, "For consider him that endured such contradiction of sinners against himself..."

The next time when you feel that you can't bear it consider Jesus and his experience with the cross. The cross was the most cruel and painful execution of Jesus' day. The cross was designed for thugs! The execution was carefully planned to put fear into all who watched. The executioners were trained to drive the nails through the hands to tear the nerves that ran from the hands into the arms. The nails through the feet were designed to literally render the victim paralyzed. They wanted the victim to have a heart attack when on the cross. The cross was extremely cruel. Even some of the victims clothes were stripped as they hung shamefully naked and exposed. What a cruel death. But Jesus endured!

Hebrews 12:3, "Consider him who endured..."

Jesus endured the cross. The word "endure" is an interesting word. It means to stand under the load. God will give you the strength to stand underneath the load. It's called endurance! This word endurance is other times translated "Patience." Not patience that sits by doing nothing but the patience that stands under the load and grows from adversity.
You will need this character trait. You need to develop this "spiritual strength" to be able to withstand against the wiles of the devil. Jesus endured the cross because he knew the purpose of God in his life. Consider Jesus and how he handled his cross.

He saw the joy that was sat before him.......

Fill you Mind with Victorious Thoughts
Hebrews 12:3, "Lest ye be wearied and faint in your minds"

The enemy attacks our minds. The battle ground is in your mind. And so the enemy tries to plant seeds of doubt and defeat within your mind. He tries to blind your mind with a poor-self image of yourself. Notice that the text says that defeat is in our mind.

Hebrews 12:3, "...Faint in your mind..."

Therefore it is important to fill your mind with "**victorious**" thoughts! Fill your mind with "**Can-Do It**" thoughts! Fill your minds with "**positive**" thoughts!

Some Victorious Scriptures:

Psalm 46:1, "God is my refuge and my strength. God is the strength of my life."

Philippians 4:13, "I can do all things through Christ that strengthens me."

1John 4:4, "Greater is he that is in you, than he that is in the world."

Psalm 27:1, "The Lord is my light and my salvation; whom shall I fear? The Lord is the strength of my life; of whom shall I be afraid?"

Think positive thoughts! Let the thoughts of God permeate your inner being. Think in terms of victory!

Philippians 4:8, "Finally, brethren, whatsoever things are true, whatsoever things are honest, whatsoever things are just, whatsoever things are pure, whatsoever things are lovely, whatsoever things are of good report think of these things."

Jimmy R. Stevens

The enemy wants entrance through your thought life. Fill up your mind with the word of God.

There is no Comparison
Hebrews 12: Ye have not resisted unto blood, striving against sin.

If you think you are the only person in your situation you will become weary and faint in your mind. But if you compare your situation with what Jesus went through, you will find that there is no comparison. Let me ask you several questions?

1) Have you ever bleed for your witness for Jesus?
2) Have you ever had to carry a heavy wooden cross up a hill?
3) Has any one ever nailed spikes in your hand?
4) Has any one ever nailed spikes in your feet?
5) Have you ever been beaten with rods on your back?
6) Has anyone ever put a thorny crown of thorns on your head?
7) Have you ever been suspended on a cross for three hours?

How did you answer these questions? Did you answer "yes" to at least one of them? Perhaps you did not answer because there is no comparison. Stop even comparing yourself with others because you don't know what they have been through!

The Suffering of Jesus
"The Mind of Christ"

The Gethsemane Ordeal

T. J. Hunt said, "As Jesus entered into Gethsemane he told Peter, James, and John, "My soul is deeply grieved to the point of death; remain here and keep watch" (Mark 14:34). The strange prayers of Gethsemane are so different from any other prayer He ever prayed that it seems almost incredible to hear Jesus say, "Abba! Father! All things are possible for Thee; remove this cup from Me; yet not what I will, but what Thou wilt" (v.36).

When we are in trauma, the capillaries in the sweat glands just under the surface of the skin dialate. You see this when people blush. If the stress is intense enough, the blood vessels pressing against the sweat glands burst. The blood has nowhere to go except out through the sweat glands, and the person sweats blood. This rare phenomenon has been observed by modern doctors. The medical name for this is hematidrosis.

Whenever hematidrosis occurs, the skin is so sensitized that the slightest touch is painful. As the skin oozes blood, the skin becomes fragile and tender. The process of sweating blood also produces marked weakness and possible shock. Although Jesus' body was robust from three years of extensive walking from the extreme north to the south of Israel, His body now entered the long ordeal of the trials and the physical abuse weakened, already sensitized to pain and highly susceptible to the ghastly rigors ahead of Him. So as He prayed, He sweated great drops of blood.

The Scourging

So many died from this punishment that was called the "half-death." From one to six lectors (Roman officers) administered the punishment, and they alternated positions during the flogging. The victim was tied to a stake. The usual instrument was a flagrum to which were attached several braided leather thongs. Horace calls it the "horrible flagellum." Knots were tied into the ends of each thong, and sheep bone or balls of lead were inserted into the knots.

Jewish whipping was limited to thirty-nine stripes. According to Deuteronomy 25:3, the legal limit was forty lashes, but the fortieth stripe was left out in case of a miscount (see 2 Cor. 11:24). Roman scourging had no set limit; its limit was the skill of the lictor, who was medically trained. The object was to bring the victim as close to death as possible. Many victims died from this punishment, and when they died no blame was attached to the lectors. They were after all, administering the half-death.

The object of the balls in the thongs was to bruise, and with deft twists of the thongs the lectors could cut open the bruises they were making. The continued lacerations tore into the underlying skeletal muscles and so ripped and cleaved the skin of the back that it hung in quivering ribbons of bleeding flesh. Blood loss would be intense, initially from the capillaries and veins, but finally from the arteries themselves as the muscles were torn open. At times, even the entrails were laid bare.

The victim normally fainted after about two and a half minutes. The lictor would walk over, count the pulse and check the respiration. If he could feel a pulse, he would continue the scourging. Nevertheless, the intense pain and excessive blood loss had set the stage for circulatory shock. The amount of blood loss contributed to the length of time the victim survived on the cross. The wording of I Peter 2:24 indicate that the scourging of Jesus was particularly harsh. Hematidrosis and its attendant adverse effects had rendered Jesus especially vulnerable to the scourging's negative effects on His circulatory system. This partially explains the short duration of Jesus' time on the cross; His blood supply was already greatly spent.

The Crown of Thorns

The Romans crowned their Caesar with laurel, but these soldiers did not use laurel. The men plaited a crown of thorns, probably from the kindling used in the fireplace of the fortress. The head is a very vascular area, and the extreme blood loss was rendered more acute as the soldiers "crowned" Jesus. They repeatedly struck Him in the face and on the head with a staff as they jeered, "Hail, King of the Jews!" (John 19:3). To add insult to injury, they spit on Him.

Roman Execution

Now began the dread preparations for the long walk to the execution site, the Place of the Skull-Golgotha (Greek version of the Aramaic Gulgata) or Calvary (Latin version of the Greek kranion, a skull). The soldiers ripped the clotted robe from the torn back and shoulders of Jesus.

Jesus had been weakened by the long walks to the various trails; lack of food, water, and sleep; severe loss of blood; and the excruciating flogging. His physical condition now was at least serious and possibly critical. The victim's arms were stretched the length of the patibulum, and this crossbar was lashed with cords to the shoulders, the arms, and the hands. The patibulum weighed between 75 and 125 pounds.

At last began the rigorous walk to the Place of the Skull. As an example to anyone who would dare to cross Rome, the victims were forced to carry the patibulum through a narrow and twisting procession that has come to be known as the Via Dolorosa ("Way of Sorrows"). Roman crucifixion was crueler than other forms, and the victims tried to hold back. The soldiers had to force the victims forward. To do this, they tied a rope around the waist. By pulling on the rope when the victim held back, they could jerk the prisoner onward. Because of the preceding protracted tortures and the extreme weakening of His forces, Jesus was undoubtedly moving very slowly and probably staggering under the enormous weight. Simon of

Cyrene, was forced to carry the cross the rest of the way-an unusual procedure in the crucifixion process. The fall drove the thorns deeper into His brow, since Jesus' arms were lashed to the patibulum and He could not brace for the fall.

The Crucifixion

The Jews hated crucifixion. They executed criminals principally by stoning and several other methods. A society of Jewish women had secured permission to give crucifixion victims a drug to deaden the pain. They did this when the procession arrived at the Place of the skull. The two thieves accepted their potion, but Jesus refused His. He wanted His mind clear and His faculties focused. He knew what He was doing.

They flung Him into the dirt, pebbles, and grime of the hillside and stretched His arms onto the patibulum. The spikes were driven, not through the palm, but through the wrist, at the heel of the hand. Ancient peoples considered the wrist to be part of the hand. A nail through the palm cannot support the weight of the body; also, by driving the nail at a precise point through the wrist, they could aggravate the median nerve.

From this point on, a never-ending trail of fire raced up and down at the victim's arms; the only relief the victim could know from this agony was death. The spikes they used were square in shape, about 5.5 inches long and about a third of an inch across the top. This nailing causes the thumb to be drawn sharply inward; it strikes the palm, and as the process continues, the fingers also are cramped sharply inward.

Several upright bars were kept planted in the Place of the Skull. This beam, the cross, was sharpened at the top, like a pencil. In each patibulum, a hollowed-out cup was carved. Using ropes and ladders, the soldiers could lift the nailed victim and implant the hollowed-out cup onto the sharpened end of the cross, like a mortise and tenon. The lifting of the body would finally sever the median nerve, creating a lightning shot of pain in the arms. Christ was placed on the center cross probably because His was the chief "crime." The titulus ("placard") describing His "crime" read, "Jesus the Nazarene, the King of the Jews" (John 19:19).

Nails were not necessary to cause death. The Egyptians, in fact, used ropes to fasten the victim to the cross, but Rome was crueler and preferred nails. The arms were nailed at ninety degrees, but in The course of hanging on the cross, the body would sag to sixty-five degrees. The weight of the body fixed certain breathing muscles in an inhalation state and hindered passive exhalation. In other words, the pectoral muscles became paralyzed and the victim discovered that he could breathe in, but he could not breathe out. The usual cause of death in crucifixion was asphyxiation and shock from the loss of blood.

If they did not nail the feet, the victim died quickly. Prior to death the victim flailed his body and irritated the guards. The Romans had discovered a way to prevent this flailing and to prolong the agony. They bent the knees to a twenty-degree angle, slammed one foot against the cross, folded the other foot over it, and drove an additional spike through the second metatarsal space of the feet. This nail injured the peroneal nerve and branches of the medial and lateral plantar nerves; the periosteum, the membrane of highly innervated connective tissue with numerous blood vessels surrounding the bones of the feet, would be stripped off, creating intense pain.

As the victim hung there, unable to breathe, tetany, a condition marked by cramps and contractions of the muscles, would set in. A profound lack of oxygen and the inability to exhale carbon dioxide causes the tetany. The victim would discover that, if he used the nail, going through the feet as a cruel step to force his body upward so that the arms once more reached a ninety-degree angle, he could breathe again. Each time Christ spoke, He had to do this.

He alternately hung by the nails in His hands until the need for oxygen forced Him to stand on the spike in His feet. This inevitably reopened the wounds in His feet, causing further loss of blood and also greatly exacerbated the wounds in His back as He slid up and

down on the rough wood of the cross. "There they crucified Him"
Luke 23:33).

As He hung there, His muscles stood out in rigid, involuntary
cramps. The difficulty of the blood flow through the body caused
headaches and possibly convulsions. His body became soaked with
perspiration. From the loss of blood and perspiration, dehydration
was extreme and thirst became intense.

Crucifixion victims also suffered the annoyance of insects drawn
to the blood and smells. Jesus had to endure hours of twisting, joint-
rending cramps, partial intermittent asphyxiation, and fiery sting in
back as He moved up and down against the timber of the cross. Pain
and shock were extreme.

Finally, about noon ("the sixth hour," Mark 15:33), came the
dread moment for which Jesus had sweated blood. By now the whole
of His Holy being was dreadfully, terribly gripped by all the filth, dirt,
and slime of our sins-a distress far worse than any of the outward,
physical anguish. God "made Him who knew no sin to be made sin
on our behalf" (2 Cor. 5:21). Jesus was now ugly. He was hideously
deformed, repugnant. He was guilty, although it was our guilt he was
bearing. He was sin.

The most terrible moment in the history of the universe had
arrived. God the Holy Father cannot gaze upon sin. God was
consistent with His perfect holiness, God had to turn away from His
only begotten Son. In this appalling moment, the perfect continuum
of ceaseless and ageless unbroken love was suddenly split by a gigantic
rip, a horrible tear in the flawless fabric of absolute love. Perfect love
was painfully torn by an awesome rupture for the first and the only
time in all eternity. Jesus was now in the hell of exile from God.

Now Jesus was isolated, dreadfully alone, guilty, and condemned.
He had to suffer this torment in utter darkness, itself a curse (Exodus
10:21-23). No other human being had ever known what He now knew
in these hour.

Normally the brain will not accept severe trauma; it blacks out.
If the brain refuses to faint for some unknown reason, the stomach
pours gastric juices and blood into the abdominal cavity. This gastric

dilatation extends from the neck to the hips. His body was now hideous, deformed into a repugnant, bloated mass. "His appearance was marred more than any man and His form more than the sons of men" (Isa. 52:14).

By this time, Jesus' heart was struggling to pump the small amount of blood left in His torn and lacerated system. In these final desperate stages, according to some medical authorities, blood serum began to engorge the pericardium, the sac of thin membrane that surrounds the chest cavity. The squeezed heart now was laboring to pump heavy, thick, sluggish blood through the maimed and sorely abused body. He paid our sin death in full. He paid entirety the enormous debt for all the sin against holiness. Jesus paid it all. The work was now over. Astonishingly, He called out His final cry from the cross in a loud voice, indicating the strength He still had. He had been in control. At the end, He was still in control. He prayed, "Father, into Thy hands I commit My spirit." (Luke 23:46). The fact that he committed His spirit indicates an act of submission. Jesus Christ breathed His last breath and gave up (John 19:30, paradidomi) His spirit. The lungs stopped their functioning, and the struggling heart finally stopped. He was dead.

The work of the cross was to atone for our sins. Without the cross, redemption would have been beyond price. Yet redemption is free through the atoning sacrifice of the Lord Jesus Christ. Holiness and love had worked together to complete the mightiest work of all eternity. God's holiness was totally satisfied. No one now could ever question His love.

Jesus really did suffer. Your suffering is no comparison. Keep the faith and don't faint! You are a special unique creation to God! And God will develop you into the likeness of his great son, Jesus Christ. Let God have His perfect work in you. The two words that the writer used for growing weary and fainting are the two words that are used for an athlete who flings himself to the ground and collapse after he has passed the winning line of the race. God does not want you to mentally or spiritually collapse. You can cross the finish line."

Questions & Answers

1) Have you made a commitment to endure?

_____

_____

_____

_____

2) Are you filling your mind with positive thoughts?

_____

_____

_____

_____

3) Can you compare your suffering with the suffering of Jesus?

_____

_____

_____

_____

4) Will you cross the finish line?

_____

_____

_____

_____

14

How to Stay In the Race
Hebrews 12:1-3
Objective: To learn the principles of endurance

Wherefore seeing we also are compassed about with so great a cloud of witnesses, let us lay aside every weight, and the sin that so easily beset us, and let us run with patience the race that is set before us. (Hebrews 12:1)

Introduction

In the summer of 2012 in London, England the entire world was tuned into the Olympic Games. Athletes from over 204 nations were assembled for these sporting competitions. Gold, silver and bronze medals were awarded. Some of the events were basketball, wrestling, boxing, baseball etc. But perhaps the most exciting of all the events were the track events. These athletes were competing in the sprints and distance races.

Just like these athletes are in a race, we Christians are also in a race. But in our race the fastest times are not the necessary requirements for winning. God desires that we develop the patience, courage and endurance in this Christian race. Today we will learn three principles that will help us to endure. There are temporal and eternal rewards waiting for you.

Look Around You
Hebrews 12:1, "Wherefore seeing we also are compassed about with so great a cloud of witnesses..."

The great cloud of witnesses (great assembly) were the heroes of faith that we studied in Hebrews Chapter eleven. It is suggested that these heroes of faith are in the grandstands in heaven looking down and cheering us on. Just like in a stadium the athletes are on the track and the people are seated in the stands. The word 'witnesses" does not mean "spectator" but means "martyr." These heroes of faith are not just cheering us on as spectators but they are there cheering us on because they have ran this race and they have endured.

One of the things that I enjoy reading are autobiographies of great people. One of my favorite television shows are the ones that give the story of celebrities. I am really fascinated by the paths that these people took to their destiny. These stories bring great strength to my heart and mind. I have noticed that each of their paths has been littered with obstacles, challenges, failures and victories. The examples around you can be motivational. Look around you there are many people that have overcome great odds to success! If they did it you can do it also!

But perhaps the greatest motivational stories of achievers are right there in the word of God. They overcame insurmountable things for the glory of God. And God wants us to draw from their experiences.

Romans 15:4, "For whatsoever things were written aforetime were written for our learning, that we through patience and comfort of the scriptures might have hope."

Abraham overcame physical limitations at the age of eighty-nine to father Isaac....

Moses overcame a speech impediment to become a great spokesman for the Lord and his people....

Sarah overcame barrenness to become the mother of a nation...

Rahab overcame the past of prostitution to become the great grandmother of King David...

King David overcame the murder by seeking the forgiveness and cleansing of God....

Gideon overcame a deep sense of inadequacy to become a mighty man of valor...

Jephthae overcame a life as a gang leader and destructive behavior to become a judge in Israel...

Samson overcame a serious moral fall to destroy more of his enemies in death than in life....

Esau overcame the anger and murder in his heart after being tricked by his brother Jacob...

Jacob overcame a life time of scheming and trickery to trusting in God to provide for his needs....

Look around you at modern realities, biblical history and draw from them the inspiration that you need to be a success in the Lord.

Look at Yourself
Hebrews 12:1, "Wherefore seeing we also are compassed about with so great a cloud of witnesses, let us lay aside every weight, and the sin which doeth so easily beset us, and let us run with patience the race that is set before us."

Now after you have looked at models of spiritual success you must look at yourself. Have you ever seen when a baseball player is on deck he has a heavy donut of iron around the bat? But when the umpire says, "You're up" he takes the weight off and goes into the batter's box ready to get a hit. In this race the author urges the readers to take off the weights:

Hebrews 12:2, "Lay aside every weight…"

Lay aside every weight! Lay aside anything and everything that is hindering you from being successful in the race. Take off the "emotional" weights! Take off the "spiritual" weights! Even take off the "physical" weights that are hindering you.

Hebrews 12:2, "And the sin which doeth so easily beset us…."

Also get rid of the "sins" in your life that are keeping you from being productive in the race. Your unconfessed sins will keep you from prospering in the Lord. Remove all that "junk" from your life! It is only hindering you. Be honest with yourself, look at yourself and make the necessary changes.

Hebrews 12:2, "And let us run the race with patience" (Perseverance)…

You are in need of patience which is also endurance and perseverance! Let the Lord build character in you and you will be strong when the challenges come into your life.

Look at Jesus
Hebrews 12:3, "Looking upon to Jesus the author and finisher of your faith; who for the joy that was set before him endured the cross, despising the shame, and is set down at the right hand of the throne of God."

We must focus on Jesus. It is when we take our eyes off of him that destructive things will come. We must look to Jesus because he is the author and completion of our faith. Jesus is our prime example and motivator because he teaches how to endure. There was no one who has ever suffered as he has suffered. He literally became sin for us! Jesus endured the cross because he saw the joy that was set before him. You can endure as a believer because there is also a joy that is set before you.

Look to Jesus because his life also teaches that after the shame, humiliation, tears and rejection that the glory will come. The glory came to Jesus after the cross. The cross seemed to be an ending but in reality it was a glorious beginning. The resurrection! And now Jesus sits in the highest seat in the universe! Every knee shall bow to Him and every tongue will confess that He is Lord! Look to Jesus and He will give you the spiritual resources that you need to endure anything!

Questions & Answers

1) What person inspires you?

_____

_____

_____

_____

2) What do you possess within that motivates you?

_____

_____

_____

_____

3) When you look at Jesus what do you see?

_____

_____

_____

_____

4) What weights are you going to put aside?

_____

_____

_____

_____